simply
window treatments

Sunset

simply
window
treatments

BY THE EDITORS OF SUNSET BOOKS

SUNSET BOOKS • MENLO PARK, CA

SUNSET BOOKS

Vice President, General Manager: Richard A. Smeby

Vice President, Editorial Director: Bob Doyle

Production Director: Lory Day

Art Director: Vasken Guiragossian

SIMPLY WINDOW TREATMENTS was produced in conjunction with
Roundtable Press, Inc.

Directors: Marsha Melnick, Susan E. Meyer, Julie Merberg

STAFF FOR THIS BOOK:

Developmental Editor: Linda J. Selden

Senior Editor: Carol Spier

Book Design: Areta Buk/Thumb Print

Technical Writer: Cyndi Marsico

Illustrations: Beverley Bozarth Colgan, Celia M. Mitchell

Photo Research: Ede Rothaus

Editorial Assistant: John Glenn

Production Coordinator: Patricia S. Williams

Cover Photograph· Jamie Hadley, *Photo Direction:* JoAnn Masaoka Van Atta;
curtains made by Suzanne Klodowski

Photography acknowledgments appear on page 128.

10 9

ISBN 0-376-01737-6

Library of Congress Catalog Card Number: 98-86297

Printed in Hong Kong

For additional copies of SIMPLY WINDOW TREATMENTS or any other *Sunset* book,
call 1-800-526-5111.

foreword

whatever the style of your home, windows are one of its principal features. If for no other reason than to create privacy, we all add some sort of covering to most of them. Generally we view this covering as a primary component of our decor. Window treatments create or enhance the character of each room, and they're easy to customize—it's wonderful how versatile a rectangle of cloth can be. *Simply Window Treatments* is an inspirational and practical guide to making curtains, shades, and swags.

Part One: Be Creative encourages you to put on your design cap and think creatively. It helps you analyze the way a window treatment will work in your decor, make design choices, and select materials. Photos of curtains, shades, and swags in different styles and settings help you visualize the possibilities and choose the window treatment that's right for you.

Part Two: Projects features a selection of great-looking curtains, shades, swags, and valances, with detailed illustrated directions for making them. Most of the designs are simple to make, a few are more complicated. Almost all will complement casual or formal settings equally well—your fabric choice will set the tone.

As you look through the projects, you'll see that several conclude with a Design Variation feature that suggests other ways you can interpret these treatments—look for these while you're in the planning stage. You'll also find special Designer Details throughout the book. These are trimming and construction techniques that add distinction; they're written generically so you can easily adapt them to other situations.

Part Three: Basics covers the general planning, measuring, estimating, cutting, and construction techniques you'll use to make any window treatment. You'll find worksheets to simplify yardage calculations here. This section also identifies and explains the equipment you should have on hand.

Whichever project you choose, we encourage you to adapt the ideas and directions to suit your windows and taste. Adjust the proportions, add or omit details, change color, fabric, and trim—be creative.

table of contents

part one
be creative   8

THINKING CREATIVELY   10
CHOOSING A TREATMENT   13
CHOOSING FABRIC   18
CHOOSING TRIM   22
INTO THE WORKROOM   23

part two
projects   24

HOW TO USE THE DIRECTIONS   26
BOUND-EDGE RING CURTAINS   28
BASIC ROD-POCKET PANELS   30
RUFFLED ROD-POCKET CURTAINS   34
CLEVER ARCH-TOP CURTAINS   40
OVERLAY TAB CURTAINS   42
SIMPLE SASH CURTAINS   46
ROLLED STAGECOACH VALANCE   49
GRACEFUL TAPERED VALANCE   52
CLASSIC SUNBURST CURTAIN   54
REVERSIBLE CUFFED CURTAIN   56
PLEATED SCALLOPED VALANCE   60
SIMPLE TIED SWAG   63
TRADITIONAL SWAG AND TAILS   66
TAILORED SCARF SWAG   72
TRIANGULAR SCARF SWAG   74
SOFT-FOLD ROMAN SHADE   76
POUFED CLOUD SHADE   80
JAUNTY BALLOON VALANCE   84
ELEGANT LONDON SHADE   87
EASY ROLL-UP SHADE   90

part three
basics   92

GETTING STARTED   94
ABOUT INSTALLATION   108
CONSTRUCTION TECHNIQUES   111
ESSENTIAL EQUIPMENT   122

INDEX   127

ACKNOWLEDGMENTS   128

designer details

ROD POCKETS AND HEADINGS   32
ROD SLEEVES   33
PETTICOAT SWAG   36
ALL-IN-ONE LINING/BORDER   37
MAKING TIEBACKS   38
SHEER MITERED HEMS   44
SPECIAL BOWS AND ROSETTES   58

design variations

TAB ALTERNATIVES   45
HOURGLASS SASH CURTAINS   48
TAILED STAGECOACH VALANCE   51
OTHER TIED SWAGS   65
SWAG AND TAIL ARRANGEMENTS   71
FLAT ROMAN SHADES   79
OTHER CLOUD SHADES   83

be creative

STAND IN AN EMPTY ROOM AND ONE OF THE FIRST things you'll notice is the windows—their shape, size, the light that enters through them. Large, small, individual, grouped, rectangular, or arched, they have enormous influence on your living space. By dressing them in cloth you link them to the rest of your decor, soften their architectural qualities, and block the view in and out. Window treatments may not be quite as permanent as the windows they dress, but their role in establishing the ambience in a room is at least as important. Whether you choose curtains, shades, or swags, you can interpret them in a style that is casual, elegant, traditional, quirky, colorful, quiet, or dramatic.

thinking creatively

most window treatments are simply rectangles of cloth that are eased, pleated, or draped over a window opening. They're easy to visualize and, once you buckle down and measure accurately, easy to plan and make. Their shape is almost always uncomplicated, so they're fun to embellish. Because they're such an important part of a room's decor, you can use window treatments to create or accent a color palette, or to establish a design style or theme. And they offer endless opportunities for showing off beautiful fabric. Before you select the specifics of your window treatment, be sure you understand its place in your overall decorating scheme. Following are some questions that will focus your thinking. You'll see that the answers work together to help you choose window treatments that will be successful in every way.

Are you decorating or redecorating? Creating a whole new ambience or just changing one or two elements? Will you be integrating your new window treatment with a new or existing decor?

What about style and ambience? What style is the architecture and does it provide the key to your decor? How dominant should the window treatment be? Do you want it to dictate the style or colors used throughout the room or act as a discreet backdrop? What kind and how much of a statement should your new curtain, swag, or shade make: Quiet? Breathtaking? Witty? Tailored? Casual? Have you considered the trims as well as the fabric?

What about decorative hardware and accessories? Not all treatments call for decorative hardware, but those that do can really be enhanced by it. Would you like poles with decorative finials? Ornamental brackets? Will the curtain slide on rings? What about holdbacks? Tiebacks? Does your taste lean toward wood? Metal? Painted? With a special decorative finish? An ornate or simple shape? The options

When closed, flat rod-pocket panels are as tailored as Roman or roller shades; tied open, they make a lively frame for the view. Note the covered buttons that hold the ties.

LEFT: Why are Roman shades so often made in solid or striped fabric? This vigorous vegetable print is an inspired choice for a kitchen—and the shades are a good solution for corner windows.

BELOW: Stripes, checks, plaids—they're clean, fresh, fun, and sometimes very sophisticated. Whether woven, like these, or printed, they come in every scale, color, and fabric imaginable.

are myriad. If you want to make curtains or scarf swags, choose your design and basic hardware styles together, then select the specific hardware to complement your architecture and fabric.

What about the windows? Are they architecturally special, making you want to show them off? Perhaps the window dressing should be installed inside the window recess so the molding is always revealed. Is the view so spectacular that creating privacy or shade is the only reason for a window covering? Perhaps a soft treatment is not the right choice—consider flat fabric shades or commercially made blinds or shutters. Are the windows problematic, making you want to camouflage them? Perhaps the treatment should be installed outside the window recess so you can visually alter the proportion. Most designs can be installed inside or outside the window recess.

What is the purpose of the window treatment? To provide a decorative accent? To focus attention on a view? To soften the architecture? To make the room look larger or smaller? To provide privacy? To darken the room for sleeping, or to shield furnishings from the bleaching rays of the sun? Will you need to combine curtains with a shade, blinds, or shutters to meet your requirements?

Should the treatment be adjustable or fixed? If you're making curtains, do you want them to draw open at the top or just be held back at the sides? If you're making a shade, do you want it to go up and down or be fixed as a valance?

thinking creatively

RIGHT: Modest proportions and ticking stripes make this double swag and tails an unpretentious yet traditional choice for a period room. The rosette is a double Maltese cross. The matchstick shade provides a complementary filter for the sun. BELOW: Jacquard fabrics come in myriad pattern styles. Take advantage of their reversible weave and let the "wrong" side show on tied-back unlined treatments.

How long do you plan to keep the window treatment? Are you decorating a child's room? A dwelling you don't plan to stay in? Do you just want to create privacy quickly until you are ready for a major redo? Or is the treatment part of a long-term decor? Answers to these questions may help you determine how much time and money you want to invest.

What sort of skills do you have? Do you consider your sewing machine friend or foe? Is it sturdy enough for the task in mind? Do you have a good steam iron? What about space? Window treatments can take yards of fabric; you'll need to spread it out in order to cut it accurately. Most of the window treatments in this book are quite easy to make, but basic sewing experience will be helpful.

This book presents many design ideas and features twenty projects with directions, plus some variations. Many of the designs can be adapted to dress a variety of windows and doorways—or you can use them for bathtubs, beds, under counters or sinks, or inside cabinet doors. Each can be interpreted in any number of fabrications with strikingly different results. To get off to a confident start, read Basics, pages 92–126, and remember that careful planning is key. There is no such thing as a "standard" window—be prepared to do your math. If your tolerance for making careful calculations is limited, select a project in a casual style where the proportions aren't too critical, and choose fabric in a solid color, vertical stripe, or with a small repeating pattern. After all, complicated is not a synonym for special, sophisticated, unique, or beautiful. So be imaginative.

choosing a treatment

when you contemplate the design possibilities for your window treatments, you will be thinking of several interdependent factors: You'll think first of the overall style of your decor and of the architecture—the shape, size, and configuration of the windows and doors you wish to dress. And you'll think about possible fabrics and the way in which their color, pattern, texture, sheen, and weight interact with the rest of your decor. The object of the design process is to devise a window treatment that fits stylishly into its surroundings. Part of this process is creative and part is practical—you want to choose a design, fabric, and trim that are aesthetically pleasing, and you want the treatment to be fixed or adjustable, as appropriate.

Floor-length white London shades pouf extravagantly when raised, are imposing when lowered. A truly handsome and unusual choice for a window wall.

choosing a treatment

Simple rod-pocket curtains in a clean
shirting stripe sit comfortably over opaque
honeycomb blinds. The tassel tiebacks
quietly complete the ensemble.

Before you can decide on the details of your
design, you'll have to make a basic decision: What
type of window treatment do you want—curtain,
shade, or swag—and do you want to combine two
components to create it? Both curtains and shades
can be made shorter than the window opening
and used as valances, or mounted to cover only
the lower portion of the opening.

What about curtains? You can hang curtain
panels over a window individually or in pairs, and
pull them open to one or both sides. The curtains
featured in this book are of two basic types: those
with a rod pocket (casing) at the top and those
with tabs or rings sewn to the top. Because a
casing will not slide easily over a pole, rod-pocket
curtain panels are stationary once they are
installed. If the panels cover the window expanse,
they can be held open with tiebacks (cloth or
cord) or holdbacks (wood or metal). If rod-pocket
panels hang at the sides of the window only, the
space between them is usually spanned with a
valance or rod sleeve. Curtains that hang from
rings or tabs are easily pulled open or closed.
Because the pole is visible, ring and tab curtains
are generally paired with decorative, but not
necessarily ornate, supporting hardware. Both
types of curtains can hang flat or with fullness.

What about shades? Shades open from the
bottom of the window to the top. There are three
basic types: those that roll up from the bottom,
called roll-up shades; those that roll up over a spring rod at the top, called
roller shades; and those that pull up into gathers or pleats by means of
cords and rings, called pull-up shades. Roll-up shades are controlled by a
cradle of cording that is visible on the front and back of the shade; they
are usually informal. Roller shades must be made from stiffened fabric so
they operate smoothly; they can be formal or informal, but usually appear
tailored. Pull-up shades offer a world of design possibilities: Roman shades
hang flat across the window and stack up in regular pleats. Cloud shades
are rod-pocket curtains that pull up to form poufed scallops. Balloon shades
have vertical pleats and pull up to form tailored scallops. London shades are
a variation on balloon shades; when raised they fall into tails and scallops.

What about swags? Swags drape across the top of a window opening. Swags are purely decorative—you can't use them to moderate the flow of light. Two types are featured in this book: traditional pleated swags, which are attached to a mounting board, and scarf swags, which are informally pleated or tied and then draped over holdbacks or brackets. Traditional swags are often used over pleated tails or over curtain panels; scarf swags form their own tails, but some styles look well atop curtains.

What about privacy and light control? If these are of concern to you, plan to line your curtains or shades with an opaque fabric or combine them with commercially made blinds, shutters, or roller shades. Sheer and translucent fabrics permit light to pass in both directions. If you can see the outdoors through them during the day, passersby will see through them into the lighted interior of your home at night. If bright sunlight streams into your home, you might want an opaque window covering—either soft or hard—to protect other furnishings from its damaging rays.

Blackout fabric is available from many home-furnishings fabric vendors and you can easily use it as a lining. Available in white or off-white, it has a rubberized coating on one side that makes it totally opaque; it is not suitable for use with sheer or semisheer fabrics. If you wish to soften the sun's rays without completely blocking it, the fabric need not be totally opaque; even sheer and translucent fabrics will filter light if they are pleated or gathered so they hang with fullness.

What about combining soft and hard window fashions? Even professional designers have a difficult time with this question, especially in traditional or period decors. How can you assure that the combination will be aesthetically

ABOVE: Cord at the top of this pretty lined panel loops casually over pegs in the window molding. Shutters provide privacy without completely darkening the room.
BELOW: Thinking of prints? Choose floral, geometric, ethnic, allover, random, small, medium, or large.

choosing a treatment

Textured fabrics make interesting window treatments. Look for patterned weaves, slubby and textured yarns, ruched or pleated effects (sometimes on prints, like the leafy pattern here), and even woven-in tassels.

pleasing? Think of the hard elements as part of the architecture, and, if possible, begin by selecting shutters or blinds that are in keeping with the style of the window. Consider also how they'll look from the outside. One trick: If the hard components supplement curtains, match their color to the fabric; if they supplement swags, valances, or adjustable shades, match the color to the window trim.

If needed only to provide privacy or darkness in a bedroom, chances are the hard elements will rarely be seen as part of the decor. In this case, contemporary miniblinds that virtually disappear when raised can be used even in a period decor. Wood and woodlike blinds and shutters—the types with adjustable horizontal vanes—are traditional complements to swags, curtains, and valances in period decors, and also suit many contemporary settings. Look not only for style, but proportion, the quality of the tape that adjusts the vanes, and color; wood blinds and shutters can of course be painted or stained. Vertical blinds do not mix well with soft treatments—their wide vanes interfere with the fabric and they really provide a complete "look" by themselves.

What should you do first? Consider all these points, and then begin your design process by collecting ideas. Collect pictures from magazines and catalogs of window fashions and rooms you find attractive. Look especially for window configurations that are similar to yours. Visit home stores and designer show houses if you can. Identify why certain ideas appeal to you— is it the way multiple shades span a wide window, or a covered pole carries color between fixed curtain panels in a bay window? Is it the layering of sheer fabrics to create multihued, translucent curtains, or the unexpected choice of a sheer for a shade? Is it the way flat curtains were folded back to create a peaked opening, or the fact that the tabs at the top of the curtains are looped over a row of pegs rather than slipped onto a pole? Is it simply the color, the fabric, the trim details? Or is it something unconventional or especially clever about the overall design? Do you understand how the effect was achieved? Will you be able to adapt it to your situation? Even if you think you want curtains rather than shades, keep an open mind while you look; you may be surprised at the ways each has been used by various designers.

The fun of design lies in deciding which details to incorporate. You may lean toward something very traditional that will stand the test of time, but as you look through this book and other decorating publications you'll see that fabrication sometimes has as much to do with the final effect as the style of the design itself. The most basic designs can be absolutely elegant in gorgeous silk with no embellishment at all; the same designs made in layers of inexpensive sheer cotton will be less formal, but not necessarily less

A large, pretty print softens tailored tab curtains. The dark wrought-iron pole is balanced by the dark lines of the mirror frame and chairs.

sophisticated. Then again, trim, tucks, or even a perfectly proportioned ruffle or bow will add interest to most designs and perhaps present a way to tie the window fashions to other elements of your decor.

Before you finalize your design, look at samples of the chosen fabric and trims in the room you are decorating. You'll want to be sure that the colors, patterns, textures, and weights look good with your other furnishings. (If you are undertaking a major decorating or redecorating task and feel insecure about creating color schemes, you'll find many good books on the subject in the decorating and art sections of bookstores and libraries.) Look at samples in both natural and artificial light. And pin them up over the window so you can see how they look with light passing through them. If you can't borrow samples from a supplier, don't economize by skipping this step—buy a piece large enough to show how the fabric works.

choosing fabric

soft window treatments are made from fabric, and fabric offers you a world of design possibilities. You may know from the outset which type of fabric you wish to use—you may even know the specific pattern. But if you don't, bear in mind that while there are times when a design concept begs to be interpreted in a specific fabric, there are other times when a fabric can suggest a design concept. Be open to both possibilities.

When you are designing it is important to think about the aesthetic as well as the practical characteristics of fabric. Fabric allows you to introduce pattern, color, and texture to your decor. *Pattern* may relate to or establish a style. When you think of styles such as country, lodge, French or English, Victorian or another period, distinct pattern images come to mind for each. *Color* establishes mood and can change your perception of space or proportion—and some palettes are associated with specific decorating styles. *Texture* contributes to the way fabric reflects or absorbs light, and thus affects its color. Fabrics can be smooth, soft, crisp, or coarse—or a combination of these. Fabrics such as bouclé, velvet, and matelassé have texture that adds dimension. The structure of a fabric's weave, the type and weight of the fiber it is made from, and the finish it is given all contribute to its texture. These

Half-curtains in a sheer moiré give a breezy finish to a room where privacy is of no concern. Tiny pleats and fabric loops march across the top edge of these panels; clip-on rings would have been another option.

latter characteristics also give each kind of fabric its *hand* (a term used to describe the way a fabric handles or behaves: how stable it is; how well it will drape, roll up, or gather; how bulky it is; and whether it will withstand the stress of any rigging) and make it suitable to use for specific types of window fashions. Additionally, the *opacity* of the fabric might be important.

Confused? Even though you may not be familiar with the jargon applied to fabrics, you can use your eyes and hands to get an idea of a fabric's suitability. Crisp fabrics do not usually drape well, nor will they undulate softly across a window. Thick fabrics can be bulky and unattractive in a pleated shade. Slippery fabrics are difficult to work with. Those with fragile surfaces will not wear well in adjustable treatments, though they might be suitable for swags. Loosely woven fabrics won't take the stress of shade rigging, but some suppliers will laminate them to a stable lining. Visit home furnishings stores to get a firsthand look at the way different fabrics are used, and be sure to handle a good-size sample of any fabric you contemplate using before you purchase it.

What kind of fabric should you use? For window treatments, home furnishings fabrics—often called *decorator fabrics*—are best. Not only do they offer great aesthetic options, but they've also been engineered to have a suitable hand, to wear well, and often to be stain resistant. Additionally, they're usually quite wide (52"–60") so they're more efficient to work with. Depending upon where you live, a wide selection of decorator fabrics may be available at your local fabric stores. If not, you can often order them through a home furnishings store or interior designer. Decorator fabrics can be very costly, and window treatments can require a surprisingly large amount of yardage. If your budget is limited, don't fall in love with a fabric that has a large pattern repeat because you're likely to need twice as much of it as you would a solid. Other good fabric options are bed linens, table linens, and, for small curtains, dish towels. Many of these have decorative

choosing fabric

Large patterns can be shown to great effect at the window. Grand patterns come in endless variety—shown here, three block prints and a toile.

hems or borders that can be shown off to great advantage. Vintage lace and linens can be used if you are not concerned about the durability of the treatment or the potential damage to the textile. In fact, when you're in need of a quick window fashion, a tension rod, some clip-on rings, and an arrangement of pretty lace or colorful linens may be perfect.

When you are considering fabrics don't confuse *fiber* with *fabric*. Fiber is what fabric is made of. Fibers are either natural—cotton, linen, silk, wool— or man-made. Some man-made fibers are created from natural materials; rayon, for example, is derived from wood. Others, such as nylon, polyester, and acrylic, are true synthetics, which are often petroleum based. The way a fiber is spun, woven, and finished determines the kind of fabric it becomes. There are a great many kinds of fabric (broadcloth, velveteen, chintz, and damask, to name just a few) and many, but not all, can be made from more than one fiber.

Decorator fabrics are often blends of several fibers. Elegant fabrics sometimes feature metallic or other novelty threads as well. Linen, rayon, and silk all add sheen and take dye well, so fabrics made with them often appear luxurious and have especially intense colors. Cotton and wool are both durable. Cotton comes in many weaves, weights, and finishes, and is easy to handle. Silk comes in many weights, textures, and finishes, and the different silks have widely varying characteristics ranging from fragile to durable and from easily handled to frustratingly slippery. Some silks water-spot easily, and a single raindrop can make them look soiled. Most silks are extremely sensitive to sunlight; they fade badly and sometimes deteriorate with constant exposure, so consider lining them. Sheers and other laces and novelty fabrics often have a high synthetic content; test a sample on your machine to be sure you can sew it without puckers.

Which fabrics will be suitable? The answer really depends upon the treatment you're making and the effect desired. At the window, anything can work. Medium-weight, nonpile, nonslippery fabrics are the easiest to work with. The more loosely woven the fabric, the less durable it will prove, so if your treatment is to be adjustable, use these fabrics with caution. If your project calls for a lining, make sure the lining is opaque enough to mask any pattern that might ghost through from the face fabric, or use an inner lining. If you must line sheers, consider lining them with themselves (a double layer of many sheer fabrics will create a pretty moiré pattern). Fabrics with plain, twill, or Jacquard and damask (motif-patterned) weaves are common choices; satin weaves are sometimes used as well. Velvets and chenilles, tapestry weaves, and some Jacquards are more difficult to work with; they're bulky and fray easily, but since most projects require only straight seams and hems, they can be used successfully. Printed fabrics usually, but not always, have a plain or twill weave. Plain and twill weaves sometimes have a glazed finish; cotton chintz is a glazed fabric often used for window treatments.

Which fabric patterns are best? Whichever style you like. Always consider the scale of the window when choosing a fabric—a small pattern on voluminous curtains will read as a solid, while a grandiose pattern might be confusing on a diminutive shade. This isn't to say that the pattern must be in scale to the window, just that you should be aware of the effect. Bear in mind that accurate yardage calculation and cutting is critical when working with patterns such as plaids, stripes, or repeating motifs, but because the pieces you'll be sewing are probably rectangles, matching these patterns won't be difficult, so don't automatically shy away from a repeating design.

What about fabric quality? Be a savvy consumer. You're about to put quite a bit of work into your project, so don't consider buying fabric that has flaws in the weave, printing, or finish, or that seems in any way to be of poor quality. Purchase your fabric from a reputable vendor. Be sure the fiber content and maintenance requirements are clearly identified. Buy all of each color or pattern from one bolt because dye lots can vary.

What about cost? Large or multiple window treatments are an investment in time and materials, and wrong choices can't be easily tossed aside. So don't take the cost lightly—if you're going to spend the time and want the treatment to wear well, it will be worthwhile to use the best fabric you can afford. If your design calls for decorative hardware (especially if you're dressing multiple windows), price it early so you won't be caught unaware.

Most curtains are simply hemmed panels of fabric; any uniqueness is due to fine points of proportion, color, or trim. These lengths of purple cloth are tacked to a mounting board, accented with bright bows, and then swagged over holdbacks.

choosing trim

fringe, decorative cording, tassels, braid, gimp, ribbon, and even sporty rickrack—trims lend polish and panache to window fashions. Trims should usually be in scale with and have the same visual weight as the fabric; however, there are times when larger or heavier trims are very effective—especially as tiebacks. You can make binding and welting and other fabric-covered cord from your principal fabric or from one that complements it. You'll find the best selection of ready-made trims in a home furnishings fabric store.

If you like trims, you're likely to find shopping for them both exhilarating and frustrating. There are so many choices, you'll no doubt be inspired to take advantage of them. But select wisely—you may be surprised by their cost. If trim is an important part of your design, be sure you can find what you want before you purchase the fabric; you may want to adjust one or the other until you find a mix that looks great and fits your budget.

Sheer lace gives a delicate touch to the usually substantial swag-and-tail design. Note the lace border finishing the edges. A discreet roller shade provides privacy.

Before committing to a trim, be sure you understand how it will be applied. Will it be inserted in a seam or topstitched to the face of the project? Will the stitching be visually disturbing on the back of the curtain or shade? Can it be sewn on by machine? Will the trim run both vertically and horizontally, and if so, is it suitable for this application? If you're planning to add vertical trim to a roll-up, roller, or Roman shade, be sure it is not overly bulky.

Most decorator trims are made of cotton, rayon, or a blend of the two. They come in myriad colors, but finding a perfect match for your fabric may prove challenging. Remember, trim is used to add interest, and one that makes a subtle or strong contrast can be more interesting than one that blends into its background. Some vendors can arrange to have trims such as tassels made to order, and many good notions retailers have a button-covering service.

into the **workroom**

be creative, be focused, be confident—let these phrases guide you through your curtain, shade, or swag making. If you gather ideas, assess the task ahead, and then take the time to plan your project, you should be able to follow through with flair.

If you are an inexperienced sewer, or haven't sewn in a while, choose a simple project and an easy-to-handle fabric for your first window treatment. On the other hand, if you're experienced and confident, you should be able to make any of the projects in this book. Whatever your experience, do take the time to read Getting Started, pages 94–107, before you begin; the planning, measuring, and yardage calculating directions given there work in tandem with the individual project directions. Professional designers and sewing contractors will be the first to tell you that the work they do before scissors meet fabric— the designing, fabric and hardware selection, measuring, and planning—can easily take as much time as the actual sewing. By spending this time, you'll ensure that the sewing goes smoothly and yields terrific results.

Cloud shades are just rod-pocket curtains gathered into scallops by means of cords and rings. This one is a valance with a small ruffle sewn to the hemline.

projects

ALMOST ANY WINDOW WILL BE ENHANCED BY THE
right curtain, swag, or shade. Following are twenty
designs—classic, eclectic, casual, elegant—with
directions. Most are simple to make and all will
assume new identities if made in different fabrics.
And because window dressings are easy to alter,
we've included numerous Design Variations. Also
check out the Designer Details—these explain
special construction processes you can use in many
ways. Throughout the directions you'll find Tips
from the Pros—hints and tricks to smooth your
work. So browse through the photos to pick a
design, read the step-by-step directions, refer to
the watercolor illustrations, and get started.

how to use the directions

Each project in this book can be made by following its illustrated step-by-step directions. To understand the components of these directions, read these two pages. Of course, every window is different—this book will help you customize the process.

1 A colored fabric panel begins each project. It contains information you need before you begin.

2 ABOUT THE SAMPLE

Here you will find a description of the treatment shown in the photo, including construction and installation basics.

3 MATERIALS

A list of materials needed, including fabrics, trims, and hardware.

✂To calculate the amount of fabric you need, refer to the planning directions further down in the panel.

4 PLANNING

This paragraph tells you how to plan the treatment and refers you to Part Three of the book, Basics, where you'll find information to help you measure, calculate yardage, sew, and install your project. Read Basics before you begin— it supports and enhances the project directions. Use the index at the end of the book to locate specific information.

5 MEASURE, MARK, AND CUT

This section reminds you to fill in the window treatment worksheets and guides you to any specific directions you must read before cutting.

6 CUTTING LIST

This names each piece needed to make the window treatment, including facings and bias strips for welting or binding, and tells you how many of each to cut.
✂The letter identifying each piece is repeated in the measuring diagram, component diagram, and directions.

7 MEASURING DIAGRAM

Before measuring, read the project directions and Part Three, Basics, and decide how you will be installing the window treatment.
✂The arrows give a general idea of where to measure. Any dashed lines indicate the perimeter of the different components of the treatment.
✂The letter on each section identifies the piece as given in the cutting list.

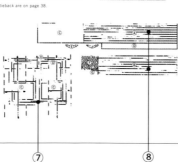

ruffled rod-pocket curtains

ABOUT THE SAMPLE
This design has stationary rod-pocket panels and a matching valance with deep headings on a separate rod. The inside panel edges and the lower valance edge are trimmed with 3"-deep ruffles; the ¾"-deep border on the ruffles binds the edge and forms a lining. The inner swag is made from a tablecloth; see the Designer Detail on page 36.

MATERIALS
Fabrics for face and ruffle lining
Thread to match
Curtain rods or poles
Mounting hardware

PLANNING
Read Inside or Outside Mount?, page 94, and Measuring for a Rod Pocket, page 99. Refer to Part Three, Basics, for information on measuring, calculating yardage, basic sewing techniques, and hardware. Decide how your curtain will be mounted; determine the proportions of each component.

MEASURE, MARK, AND CUT
Fill in the window treatment worksheets, page 104. Refer to the Designer Detail on page 37 to measure and cut the ruffles and lining/borders; cut as many strips as needed.

RUFFLES
RUFFLE LINING/BORDERS
(C) **PANEL** ✂cut as many whole and partial widths as needed for each panel
(D) **VALANCE** ✂cut as many whole and partial widths as needed for each valance
(E) **TIEBACK** ✂cut 2 for each
(F) **BIAS STRIP** ✂cut 1½"–2" deep, enough to rim each tieback
(G) **TIES** ✂cut 2, 1½" x 10", for each tieback

TIPS FROM THE PROS
✂If using heavy fabrics, consider lining the entire panel and valance, instead of just the ruffles, to prevent sagging (refer to Basics, page 119).
✂In the following illustrations, the headings on the curtain panels are optional—omit them if you wish.
✂Note that the curtain and valance are perpendicular to one another. If using a directional fabric, be sure to cut the components so the pattern hangs as you wish.
✂You can omit the border and lining from the ruffles - just be sure to include a hem allowance when planning their cut size. Alternatively, cut them twice the finished depth and fold the strips lengthwise to make a self-lining.

NOTE: The directions that follow are for making one curtain panel, and one valance. Repeat the appropriate directions for each additional element you want to make; if making pairs of panels, be sure to sew ruffles to opposite edges. Before beginning the panels or valance, sew together whole and partial fabric widths as needed. The directions for the tieback are on page 38.

RUFFLES
1 Referring to the Designer Detail on page 37, prepare a lined strip for the ruffle (A and B) for each component of your design.
✂If omitting the border and lining, sew together the ruffle strips and hem their bottom and side edges.

2 Gather the upper edge of each ruffle strip (refer to Basics, page 114). ▽

PANEL
1 Hem the outside side edge and the lower edge of the panel (C), mitering the corner (refer to Basics, page 114). ▽

2 Adjust the gathers on the panel ruffle (A/B) so that the gathered edge is ½" shorter than the unhemmed (inside) side edge of the panel.

3 With the right sides together and cut edges aligned, pin the ruffle to the unhemmed side edge of the panel; do not extend the ruffle into the top turn-in allowance. Sew the ruffle in place. Press the ruffle away from the panel as you press the seam allowance toward the panel.

4 Finish the cut edges of the seam allowance (refer to Basics, page 112).

5 Add together your rod-pocket depth, your heading depth, if any, and the ¾" hem allowance and stitching margin. On the front of the panel, mark a line this distance below and parallel to the top edge (refer to the Designer Detail on page 32).

6 Fold ½" to the wrong side along the upper edge of the panel and press. Fold fabric to the wrong side again along the marked line and press. Topstitch through all layers along the first fold. Measure, mark, and topstitch the heading, if any. ▷

7 Slip the rod through the pocket, gathering the fabric evenly. Mount the rod.

TIPS FROM THE PROS
✂Stitch the rod pocket just up to the adjacent ruffle seamline; don't stitch across the ruffle.

Ruffled curtains need not be floral. Try solids, funky fruits, or even lace fabric.

VALANCE
1 Adjust the gathers on the valance ruffle (A/B) so that the gathered edge fits the lower edge of the valance (D) between the side hem allowances.

2 With the right sides together and cut edges aligned, pin the ruffle to the lower edge of the valance; do not extend the ruffle into the side hem allowances. Sew the ruffle in place. Press the ruffle away from the valance as you press the seam allowance toward the valance.

3 Finish the cut edges of the seam allowance (refer to Basics, page 112).

34

34

8 COMPONENT DIAGRAMS

A diagram is given of each element needed to make one of each component in the treatment. For instance, in this example, one piece is shown for the curtain panel, one for the valance, one for the tieback, and one for the tieback lining. The diagrams for ruffles and bias strips show sufficient pieces to trim one panel and one valance.

✂ The diagrams are drawn in proportion to the window measuring diagram and the treatment shown in the photo. Space limitations do not always permit the component diagrams to be shown at the same scale as the window measuring diagram. Your window will be different and your pieces will be of different proportions.

✂ The letter on each piece identifies the piece as given in the cutting list.

9 STEP-BY-STEP DIRECTIONS

To make it easy to keep your place, each step of the directions is numbered. Review the information in the colored fabric panel, cut out your window treatment pieces, and then follow the directions in the sequence given. Read the directions through before beginning to be sure you understand the nature of the project.

✂ The first time a piece is handled, it is identified by letter as well as by name.

✂ If a step is illustrated, an arrow at the end of the step points to the pertinent illustration. The illustration can be above, below, or next to the text.

✂ If a technique or process is more fully explained in Part Three, this information is cross-referenced within the numbered steps.

10 TIPS FROM THE PROS

Throughout the project directions, we've included hints, tips, and words of wisdom to smooth your work. These usually follow the step to which they pertain, so read the step and the subsequent tips before proceeding.

11 DESIGNER DETAILS

Several of the projects in this book are enhanced by special "designer details." Each has been placed under a colored fabric flag and explained with extra attention to ensure that you'll be able to sew it successfully.

✂ The use of these details is by no means limited to the ways in which we've featured them. The flags make it easy for you to see the details separately from the projects, and we encourage you to think of other ways to use them—so be creative.

12 DESIGN VARIATIONS

By slightly altering the way in which some window treatments are cut, sewn, or rigged, you can create different looks. You'll find ideas for variations following a number of the projects. Look for these before beginning—and feel free to create new looks of your own.

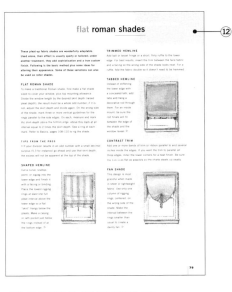

TWO IMPORTANT NOTES

✂ The standard seam allowance for sewing decorating projects is $1/2$".

✂ Any measurements given in the measuring note, cutting list, or step-by-step directions reflect those used to make the sample in the photo. Check and adjust the proportions to suit your fabric or window.

ring curtains

A contrasting binding adds interest to otherwise plain curtains.

ABOUT THE SAMPLE

These unlined curtains were made from printed linen. Each edge has a 3"-deep contrasting binding. The panels hang from rings hand-stitched to the upper edge and puddle on the floor.

MATERIALS

Fabrics for curtain and binding
Thread to match
Curtain rod or pole
Mounting hardware
Curtain rings

PLANNING

Read Inside or Outside Mount?, page 94, and decide how your curtain will be mounted. Refer to Part Three, Basics, for information on measuring, calculating yardage, basic sewing techniques, and hardware. Decide on the length, width, and fullness.

MEASURE, MARK, AND CUT

Fill in the window treatment worksheets, page 104. Refer to step 1 of the project directions to measure and cut the binding strips.

Ⓐ **TOP & BOTTOM BINDING STRIPS** ✂cut 2 for each panel

Ⓑ **SIDE BINDING STRIPS** ✂cut 2 for each panel

Ⓒ **PANEL** ✂cut as many whole and partial widths as needed for each panel

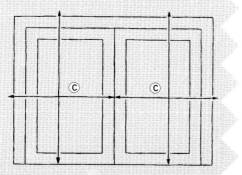

TIPS FROM THE PROS

✂If you'd like to line this curtain, cut and piece the lining fabric to the same size as each panel. Place the lining and face fabric wrong sides together, staystitch around the perimeter, and then treat the two layers as one when you apply the binding.

NOTE: The directions that follow are for making one curtain panel. Repeat the directions for each additional panel you want to make. Before beginning, sew together whole and partial fabric widths as needed.

1 Measure and cut the binding strips (A) and (B), making each one 4 times the desired finished width.
✂Cut the top and bottom strips as long as the width of the panel (C) plus 1".
✂Cut side strips the length of the panel plus 1".

TIPS FROM THE PROS

✂You can cut binding strips on the lengthwise straight grain or on the bias, but, to avoid seams on the horizontal bindings, don't cut them on the crosswise grain unless your curtain panel is narrower than the binding fabric.

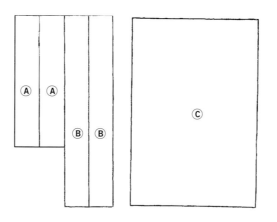

✂With a nondirectional fabric, your border will look the same on all edges.
✂If you choose a stripe or plaid, consider cutting it on the bias. Otherwise, place the stripes parallel to each edge of the panel.

2 Press the binding strips in half lengthwise, right side out. Open them and press the cut edges to the creaseline.

TIPS FROM THE PROS

✂To prepare the binding so that you'll be able to topstitch it invisibly, make one half a little wider than the other. In the following steps, align and sew the narrower half to the right side of the panel and fold the wider half over to the back; pin. Then, from the front, stitch in the ditch of the previous seam, catching the binding on the back.
✂To save on fabric, cut the binding to twice the finished width plus 1" for seam allowances. Press under 1/2" along each long edge, then press in half lengthwise. On the right side of the curtain panel, mark a line parallel to and 1/2" less than the finished width of the binding inside each edge. When you do the next step, align the cut edge of the binding with the marked line instead of with the cut edge of the panel, being sure to place the binding inside the marked line, not in the margin.

3 Unfold the top and bottom bindings along one edge and, with right sides together and cut edges aligned, pin one to the top edge of the panel, one to the bottom edge. Sew the bindings to the panel, stitching along the crease. Trim the binding ends even with the panel.

4 Fold the bindings to the wrong side of the panel, encasing the edge; pin. Secure the binding by hand or machine. ▽

5 Stitch the side bindings to the panel sides, folding in the ends instead of trimming them off. ▽

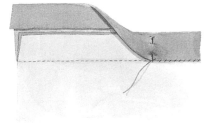

6 Decide the spacing for your rings, then divide the panel width by the spacing width; round off to the nearest whole number to find the number of spaces. The number of rings is equal to the number of spaces plus 1.

Tone-on-tone unlined printed linen is a lovely, patterned filter for the sunlight. The colored binding adds just the right contrast.

7 On the wrong side, measure along the upper edge of the panel and mark the spacing with pins; also put a pin at each upper corner.

8 Position a curtain ring at each pin, placing the lower edge of the ring on the upper edge of the binding. The eyelet or secondary ring should lie flat against the binding. Hand sew the eyelet or secondary ring to the binding. △

TIPS FROM THE PROS
✂ If your curtain rings don't have eyelets, pass a piece of narrow twill tape through each, fold the tape into a loose loop, and then sew the bottom of the loop to the binding. The loops permit the rings to twist so the top edge of the curtain hangs perpendicular to them. ▷

9 Slip the rings onto the rod.

rod-pocket panels

ABOUT THE SAMPLE

Each window in this bay is flanked by a pair of stationary rod-pocket panels that extend just to the floor; there is a ruched rod sleeve between the panels. The pole finials have matching covers. The fabric is a cotton print.

MATERIALS

Fabric

Thread to match

Curtain rod or pole with large finials

Mounting hardware

PLANNING

Read Inside or Outside Mount?, page 94, and Measuring for a Rod Pocket, page 99. Refer to Part Three, Basics, for information on measuring, calculating yardage, basic sewing techniques, and hardware. Decide how your curtain will be mounted. Decide on the length, width, and fullness, and the rod-pocket depth.

MARK, MEASURE, AND CUT

Read step 1 of the finial cover directions. Fill in the window treatment worksheets, page 104.

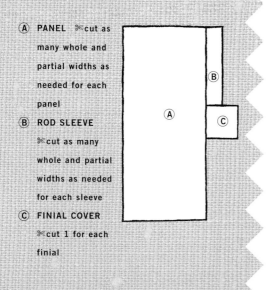

Ⓐ **PANEL** ✂cut as many whole and partial widths as needed for each panel

Ⓑ **ROD SLEEVE** ✂cut as many whole and partial widths as needed for each sleeve

Ⓒ **FINIAL COVER** ✂cut 1 for each finial

TIPS FROM THE PROS

✂Although the window treatment in the photo has no heading, you can easily add one to your curtains and/or rod sleeves. Read the Designer Details on pages 32 and 33 to see how.

✂If you are dressing multiple windows, make a separate treatment for each one, or slit the back of the rod pocket to accommodate the brackets.

NOTE: The directions that follow are for making one curtain panel, one rod sleeve, and one finial cover. Repeat the appropriate directions for each additional element you want to make. Before beginning, sew together whole and partial fabric widths as needed.

PANEL

1 Hem the vertical and lower edges of the panel (A), mitering the corners (refer to Basics, page 114).

2 Add together your rod-pocket depth, your heading depth, if any, and the ³/₄" hem allowance and stitching margin. On the front of the panel, mark a line this distance below and parallel to the top edge (refer to the Designer Detail on page 32).

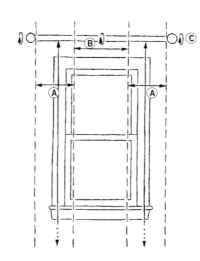

3 Fold ¹/₂" to the wrong side along the upper edge of the panel and press. Fold the fabric to the wrong side again along the marked line and press. Topstitch through all layers along the first fold. Measure, mark, and topstitch the heading, if any. ▷

SLEEVE

Referring to the Designer Detail on page 33, make the rod sleeve (B). Incorporate a heading if desired. ▽

TIPS FROM THE PROS

✂You may find it easier to make several short sleeves instead of one long one.

HANGING

1 Install the brackets and rod or pole. Don't install the finials.

2 Slip the rod through the rod sleeve and arrange the fabric at the center of the rod, gathering it evenly.

3 Inserting the rod through the pockets, slide a panel onto each end of the rod; butt the leading end of each panel against the rod sleeve.

4 Arrange the fabric in even gathers along the full length of the pole. Adjust the position of the sleeve and panels as necessary.

✄ If you are dressing multiple windows, continue to add rod sleeves and panels to the rod as appropriate to your design.

FINIAL COVER

1 Calculate the size to cut the finial cover. Finials that have sharp points or concave sides are difficult to cover. If you wish to do so, first round out the problem areas with padding—you can tape it in place.

✄ For a ball finial, use a square about 3" longer on each side than the circumference of the ball.

✄ For a double-ball or egg-shaped finial, measure from base to base over the tip of the finial. Use a square about 3" longer on each side than this dimension.

2 Install the finials.

3 Center the wrong side of the cover (C) against the end of the finial and smooth the fabric down over it, gathering it at the finial base. Secure the fabric tightly with a rubber band, piece of elastic, or sturdy string. Arrange the fabric evenly around the finial. ▽

4 Trim the fabric so that it extends about 1" over the panel pocket; notch the extending fabric as needed to reduce bulk.

5 Tuck the extending fabric neatly inside the panel pocket to conceal it.

TIPS FROM THE PROS

✄ You can conceal the elastic or string that secures the cover with a narrow strip of matching fabric.

As proof that a pretty fabric needs no special embellishment to become a stunning window treatment, the components framing this bay window couldn't be simpler—plain panels, rod sleeves, and finial covers.

rod pockets and headings

A rod pocket is a casing in a curtain that slides over a supporting rod or pole. A heading is an optional extension above the pocket (or below it when there is a lower rod); it forms a ruffle when the curtain is gathered on the rod or pole.

CHOOSING THE LOOK

Decide whether your curtain will have a shallow or deep heading or no heading at all. ▽

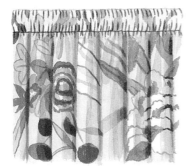

MAKING A ROD POCKET AND HEADING

1 Read Measuring for a Rod Pocket, page 99. Note the dimensions of your pocket depth, pocket allowance, heading depth, and heading allowance or keep your measuring diagram handy.

2 Hem the side edges of your curtain.

3 On the right side of the fabric, measure and mark a line $1/2$" below the upper edge. Mark another line below the first one at a distance equal to the pocket depth plus $1/4$" for the stitching margin, plus the heading depth, if any. ▽

4 With the wrong sides together, fold down the upper edge along the first line and press. Fold down along the second line and press again. Topstitch along the first fold, then brush away the markings. ▽

5 If you've planned for a heading, measure down from the second fold a distance equal to the heading depth; mark across the panel, then topstitch and brush away the markings. ▽

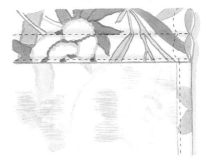

TIPS FROM THE PROS

✄ For a tailored or delicate effect, try a tiny heading—$1/8$"–$1/2$" deep—which will give a nice finish without creating a true ruffle.

A fabric-covered pole and finials have great presence but don't distract the eye from the overall impact of a window dressing. Here the fabric and colored walls are important enough; they don't warrant fancy hardware.

rod **sleeves**

When rod-pocket panels hang at the sides of the window and there is no valance, consider using a rod sleeve to bridge the gap between the panels. Generally, the sleeve gets the same heading (or lack of one) as the panels. You can also include a heading below the sleeve. ▽

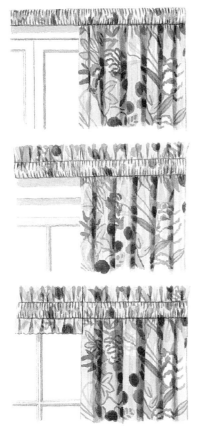

TIPS FROM THE PROS

✄Let your eye guide you in planning rod-sleeve design—you can omit the heading from the sleeve even if the panels have a heading.

PLANNING AND SIZING

Plan your sleeve to have the same fullness ratio (2:1, 2½:1, or 3:1) as the panels. The following method of determining yardage gives an even fullness across the rod.

1 Multiply the rod length by the chosen fullness ratio and subtract the finished width (flat measurement) of the side panels. Divide the remainder by the usable fabric width to arrive at the number of widths needed for the sleeve.

2 The depth (vertical measurement) of the cut sleeve is equal to the rod-pocket allowance plus the allowance for each heading, if any, plus 1" for seam allowances (refer to Basics, page 99). Match the pattern on the sleeve horizontally to the curtain panels; be sure to plan the placement of the sleeve at the appropriate part of the fabric repeat when calculating yardage.

MAKING A ROD SLEEVE

1 Sew together the fabric widths as needed. Press the seams open.

2 Make a narrow hem on each side edge.

3 Fold the fabric in half lengthwise with right sides together, aligning the cut edges, and stitch the seam. Press the seam open, using only the tip of your iron to avoid pressing creases along the edges of the inside-out sleeve. Turn the sleeve right side out.

TIPS FROM THE PROS

✄Try this trick to turn a narrow tube right side out: Guide a string through the tube with a safety pin; pin the string and tube together at one end. Then pull the string out from the other end—the tube will turn over the pinned string. Unpin and pull out the string.
✄Once the sleeve is turned right side out, center the seam on the back of the tube. Press creases only on any heading fold(s). If there is no heading, don't press sharp folds; just steam the sleeve lightly.

4 Center the seam on the back and press. ▽

5 Mark and stitch the headings as planned.
✄For a single heading, mark and stitch parallel to the upper fold at a distance equal to the heading depth (mark and stitch parallel to the lower fold if appropriate). ▽

✄For a double heading, mark and stitch parallel to both edges. ▽

6 Slip the rod through the pocket, and arrange the fabric in even gathers.

TIPS FROM THE PROS

✄Another—and very easy—way of covering an exposed section of rod is to wrap wide bias strips around it barber-pole style. Before wrapping, press under each strip edge that will be exposed. Affix the ends of the strip with glue.

rod-pocket curtains

ABOUT THE SAMPLE

This design has stationary rod-pocket panels and a matching valance with deep headings on a separate rod. The inside panel edges and the lower valance edge are trimmed with 3"-deep ruffles; the 3/4"-deep border on the ruffles binds the edge and forms a lining. The inner swag is made from a tablecloth; see the Designer Detail on page 36.

MATERIALS

Fabrics for face and ruffle lining
Thread to match
Curtain rods or poles
Mounting hardware

PLANNING

Read Inside or Outside Mount?, page 94, and Measuring for a Rod Pocket, page 99. Refer to Part Three, Basics, for information on measuring, calculating yardage, basic sewing techniques, and hardware. Decide how your curtain will be mounted; determine the proportions of each component.

MEASURE, MARK, AND CUT

Fill in the window treatment worksheets, page 104. Refer to the Designer Detail on page 37 to measure and cut the ruffles and lining/borders; cut as many strips as needed.

Ⓐ **RUFFLES**

Ⓑ **RUFFLE LINING/BORDERS**

Ⓒ **PANEL** ✂cut as many whole and partial widths as needed for each panel

Ⓓ **VALANCE** ✂cut as many whole and partial widths as needed for each valance

Ⓔ **TIEBACK** ✂cut 2 for each

Ⓕ **BIAS STRIP** ✂cut 1½"–2" deep, enough to make piping to rim each tieback

Ⓖ **TIES** ✂cut 2, 1½" x 10", for each tieback

TIPS FROM THE PROS

✂If using heavy fabrics, consider lining the entire panel and valance, instead of just the ruffles, to prevent sagging (refer to Basics, page 119).

✂In the following illustrations, the headings on the curtain panels are optional—omit them if you wish.

✂Note that the curtain and valance are perpendicular to one another. If using a directional fabric, be sure to cut the components so the pattern hangs as you wish.

✂You can omit the border and lining from the ruffles—just be sure to include a hem allowance when planning their cut size. Alternatively, cut them twice the finished depth and fold the strips lengthwise to make a self-lining.

NOTE: The directions that follow are for making one curtain panel and one valance. Repeat the appropriate directions for each additional element you want to make; if making pairs of panels, be sure to sew ruffles to opposite edges. Before beginning the panels or valance, sew together whole and partial fabric widths as needed. The directions for the tieback are on page 38.

RUFFLES

1 Referring to the Designer Detail on page 37, prepare a lined strip for the ruffle (A and B) for each component of your design.

✂If omitting the border and lining, sew together the ruffle strips and hem their bottom and side edges.

2 Gather the upper edge of each ruffle strip (refer to Basics, page 112). ▽

PANEL

1 Hem the outside side edge and the lower edge of the panel (C), mitering the corner (refer to Basics, page 114). ▽

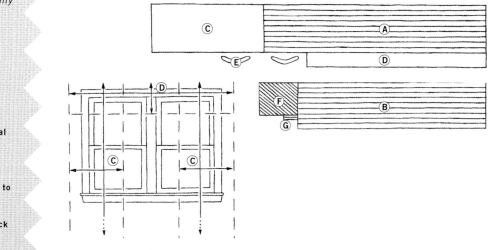

2 Adjust the gathers on the panel ruffle (A/B) so that the gathered edge is ¹/₂" shorter than the unhemmed (inside) side edge of the panel.

3 With the right sides together and cut edges aligned, pin the ruffle to the unhemmed side edge of the panel; do not extend the ruffle into the top turn-in allowance. Sew the ruffle in place. Press the ruffle away from the panel as you press the seam allowance toward the panel. ▽

4 Finish the cut edges of the seam allowance (refer to Basics, page 112).

5 Add together your rod-pocket depth, your heading depth, if any, and the ³/₄" hem allowance and stitching margin. On the front of the panel, mark a line this distance below and parallel to the top edge (refer to the Designer Detail on page 32).

6 Fold ¹/₂" to the wrong side along the upper edge of the panel and press. Fold the fabric to the wrong side again along the marked line and press. Topstitch through all layers along the first fold. Measure, mark, and topstitch the heading, if any. ▷

Ruffled curtains need not be floral. Try solids, funky fruits, or even lace fabric.

TIPS FROM THE PROS
✂Stitch the rod pocket just up to the adjacent ruffle seamline; don't stitch across the ruffle.

7 Slip the rod through the pocket, gathering the fabric evenly. Mount the rod.

VALANCE

1 Adjust the gathers on the valance ruffle (A/B) so that the gathered edge fits the lower edge of the valance (D) between the side hem allowances.

2 With the right sides together and cut edges aligned, pin the ruffle to the lower edge of the valance; do not extend the ruffle into the side hem allowances. Sew the ruffle in place. Press the ruffle away from the valance as you press the seam allowance toward the valance.

3 Finish the cut edges of the seam allowance (refer to Basics, page 112).

ruffled rod-pocket curtains

4 Fold the valance side hem allowances to the wrong side, enclosing the ends of the ruffle seam. Sew the side hems. ▷

5 Add together your rod pocket depth, your heading depth, and the ³/₄" hem allowance and stitching margin. On the front of the panel, mark a line this distance below and parallel to the top edge (refer to the Designer Detail on page 32).

6 Fold ¹/₂" to the wrong side along the upper edge of the panel and press. Fold the fabric to the wrong side again along the marked line and press. Topstitch through all layers along the first fold. Measure, mark, and topstitch the heading.

7 Slip the rod through the pocket, gathering the fabric evenly. Mount the rod.

---

petticoat swag

If you're not beginning with a tablecloth, you may want to add lace, fringe, or a ruffle to the sides of the triangle.

The swag peeking from beneath the ruffled valance on page 35 is an almost-instant project—especially if you begin with a corner cut from a pretty tablecloth (this one has deeply serrated cutwork edges). It hangs on a separate curtain rod, in this case a tension rod inside the window reveal.

Whether the fabric comes from a ready-made item or right off the bolt, you'll need a 90-degree triangular piece with two equal sides—the hypotenuse should be at least 1¹/₂ times the window width and cut on the bias.

TIPS FROM THE PROS

⊱The longer the hypotenuse, the greater the cascade effect in the draping.
⊱If you begin with a small tablecloth, cut it in half diagonally—you'll be able to make two swags. From a large cloth, cut off each corner and make four swags.

1 Make a rod pocket on the hypotenuse edge of the triangle. Slip the rod through the pocket and mount the rod.

2 Pinch a horizontal fold into the fabric about halfway between the point and the rod. Lift the fold up to the rod and pin it to the rod pocket. ▽

3 Step back and look at the swag. Adjust the drape by repositioning the fold or adding more folds.

4 If the top of the swag will be visible, neaten the folds and tack them in place; otherwise just secure them with safety pins.

TIPS FROM THE PROS

⊱If you're using a tension rod, place it as close as possible to the top of the window reveal. Then just lift the fabric and tuck it between the rod and the reveal; it will probably stay in place.
⊱For a variation on this theme, fold a square of fabric (such as a European pillow sham) in half diagonally and stitch a rod pocket along the fold. You probably won't want to drape this swag, but it will look as pretty from outside as it does in your room.

all-in-one **lining/border**

To give a ruffle a contrasting finish that looks attractive from inside or outside, use a single piece of fabric to bind the lower edge and extend up the back to form a lining. This technique duplicates the effect of a double lined ruffle without adding the extra bulk of the second lined ruffle—the fewer the thicknesses of gathered fabric, the easier it is to sew on a ruffle.

CHOOSING THE LOOK

Consider the proportions of your design, then decide whether your ruffles will have a shallow or deep border. Choose a contrasting solid or complementary patterned fabric.

TIPS FROM THE PROS

✂ If you are using a plaid or stripe, consider cutting either the ruffle or the lining/border on the bias.

For a different take on this trim, make the ruffle from contrasting fabric and bind it with the panel fabric. Add a miniature version to the tiebacks, too.

MAKING THE LINING/BORDER

1 Refer to your project schematic as you determine the proportions for the ruffles. Cut the ruffle and lining strips as follows, being sure to cut enough to trim each component in your design.

✂ To find the depth to which to cut the ruffle strips (A), determine the depth of the finished ruffle, including the border, and add 1/2" seam allowance for sewing the ruffle to the panel or valance. Cut as many strips as are needed to create a ruffle of the desired fullness.

✂ To find the depth to which to cut the lining/border strips (B), add 2 times the desired border depth to the cut depth of the ruffle strips. Cut a lining strip for each ruffle strip. ▽

TIPS FROM THE PROS

✂ If you wish, you can omit the lining and just bind the edge of a ruffle (refer to Basics, pages 115–16). For best results, use a lightweight fabric.

2 Sew together the ruffle pieces to make one long strip. Press the seams open; it is not necessary to finish the edges. Sew together the lining strips in the same manner.

3 Determine which long edge of the ruffle is to be bordered. Parallel to this edge and the depth of the border inside it, mark a line on the wrong side of the ruffle. This line is the seamline for attaching the border.

TIPS FROM THE PROS

✂ If your border depth is equal to one of the seam guides on your sewing machine throat plate, it's not necessary to mark the seamline on the ruffle. Just identify the edge to be sewn to the lining.

4 With the right sides together and aligning the marked ruffle edge with one long edge of the lining, pin and sew the ruffle to the lining on the marked line. ▽

5 Press the seam allowance toward the lining.

6 From the strip, cut a piece long enough to be gathered to fit the component edge that will receive a ruffle. Repeat as appropriate for your design.

7 On each piece, press 1/2" at each end to the wrong side. ▽

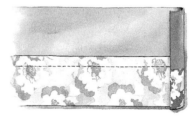

8 Fold the lining to the wrong side of the ruffle, aligning the long cut edges so the border forms along the edge of the ruffle. Pin the cut edges together. Pin and edgestitch or slipstitch the ends. ▽

making tiebacks

Whether the look is dressy, tailored, informal, or eclectic, it's best to keep tiebacks simple so they don't dominate the overall effect. How to measure? Wrap your tape measure around the curtain panel in a gentle embrace, bring the tape together, and swing it to the molding or wall where you'll attach a hook. Here are some design ideas with general directions; refer to Part Three, Basics, if you need specific sewing help.

LINED SHAPED TIEBACK

A gently curved tieback will hang more gracefully than a straight one—the deeper (vertically) a straight tieback is, the more it will flare away from the curtain at the top edge. This tieback can be attached to the wall with ties, like those shown on page 35, or small rings, as you wish. For rings, the tieback embrace should be long enough to reach the wall; for ties, it can be shorter. ▽

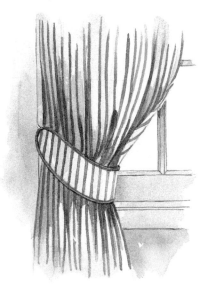

1 Fold a piece of paper or muslin in half and on it, extending from the fold, draw a rectangle half as long as the required tieback embrace and about twice as deep as the tieback. Within the rectangle, draw a curved line from the midpoint of the fold to the opposite top corner.

Sketch in a second line the depth of the tieback below the first, rounding it inside the corner. Refine the shape and cut out the pattern (piece E on page 34) through both layers. ▽

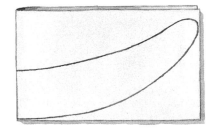

2 Test the fit of the pattern. Adjust the size and shape as necessary. For each tieback, cut one piece from the face fabric and one from the lining, adding seam allowance all around. Interface the pieces if you want them to be crisp.

3 If desired, sew matching or contrasting piping (piece F on page 34) and/or a ruffle—the tieback in the photo on page 35 has both—to the right side of the face fabric piece, finishing the ends neatly. Sew a tie (or a pair of ties) at each end if appropriate.

TIPS FROM THE PROS

✂ Tiebacks look great with bound edges. Cut the pieces without seam allowance, baste them, wrong sides together, and then bind the edges.

4 With the right sides together, pin and sew the face fabric to the lining; leave an opening on the lower edge. Trim the seam allowance as necessary. Turn the tieback right side out. Press, turning the seam allowance on the opening to the inside, and slipstitch the opening closed.

5 If you did not use piping, sew trim such as rickrack or ribbon around the perimeter.

6 If you did not attach ties, sew a ring on the wrong side of the tieback at each end. Alternatively, sew ties to the right side, tying a decorative knot in the tie where you sew it on.

TIPS FROM THE PROS

✂ Tiebacks have a front and back end. The back end is the end that goes behind the curtain.
✂ When using rings, position the front ring just inside the end, center the back ring over the edge; whipstitch over the arc closest to the middle of the tieback.
✂ When sewing trim to a tieback, begin and end at the back end so the joining seam can be placed toward the glass.
✂ You can contour the lower edge of a shaped tieback however you like—scallops and zigzags are two options.

RUCHED TIEBACK

It's not necessary to reserve these for formal designs. They look terrific made from informal sheers such as scrim or organza—try several layers together. ▽

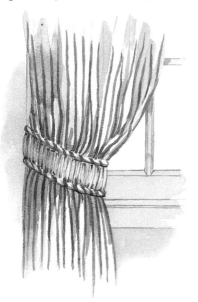

1 For each tieback, cut two bands of lining the length and depth desired for the tieback, plus seam allowance. Interface one band if desired. From the ruche fabric, cut a bias strip the same depth and 2$\frac{1}{2}$–3 times as long as the lining bands.

2 Gather both long edges of the bias strip. Place it, right side up, on one of the lining pieces (the one with the interfacing) and adjust the gathers so the bias is the same length as the lining. Baste along the edges. Sew piping to the right side of both long edges or all the way around.

3 Complete steps 3, 4, and 6 of the Lined Shaped Tiebacks, opposite, and read the tips that follow them.

TIPS FROM THE PROS

✂ The bias edge won't ravel. Here is another way to make a ruched tieback that is especially pretty in taffeta or another reversible lightweight fabric: Make a lined or turned band of fabric in the desired size. Cut the bias strip to the finished depth (pinking shears are a pretty option) and 2$\frac{1}{2}$–3 times the finished length, and gather $\frac{1}{2}$" inside each long edge. Adjust the gathers to fit the band, and topstitch the bias in place along the gathers.

TIED SASH

A long band of fabric wrapped around the curtain and tied in a bow or knot is a simple and often very effective tieback. Your choice of fabric and the way you tie it makes a sash elegant, casual, or whimsical.

A sash can be lined or unlined, but both sides will show, so lining is your best option unless you want to finish the edge with a tiny rolled hem or a decorative serger stitch. ▽

1 Cut an appropriately proportioned strip of fabric on the straight grain or bias; cut a matching or contrasting strip for lining. Cut the ends of the strips on an angle.

2 If you wish, sew matching or contrasting piping to the right side of one strip, beginning and ending in the middle of one long edge.

3 Complete step 4 of the Lined Shaped Tieback, opposite.

4 Sew a ring to the middle of the right side of the sash. Place the ring over the hook on the window trim, and wrap and tie the sash around the curtain.

TIPS FROM THE PROS

✂ Play with stripes or plaids—cut either the sash or the piping on the bias.
✂ Bind the edges instead of using piping.
✂ Sew ribbon or rickrack around the perimeter.
✂ Be creative with sheers—use several layers together or use a single layer and give it a decorative edge finish.
✂ Make the sash extra deep so it crushes as you wrap it. Make it extra long and wrap it several times before tying.
✂ Instead of sewing on trim, just lay decorative cords over the sash; wrap and tie them together.
✂ To easily maintain the bow, make the sash in two pieces, sew a curtain ring to one end of each, hang them, and then tie a bow. When you want to release the curtains, just unhook one of the rings and let the tied sash hang behind the curtain panel.

arch-top curtains

ABOUT THE SAMPLE

The top edge of these simple curved-top curtains is trimmed with a thick pile cord. Loops set into the top seam slip onto hooks on a custom rod—you can alternatively use decorative hooks or pegs set into your molding or wall. Each lightweight silk panel has a lining set flush with the edges.

MATERIALS

Fabrics for curtain and lining

Decorative cord, welting, or other trim, with or without a flange

Thread to match

Decorative hooks (curved rod, holdbacks, and hardware are optional)

PLANNING

Read Inside or Outside Mount?, page 94, and Arched Curtains, page 101. Refer to Part Three, Basics, for information on measuring, calculating yardage, basic sewing techniques, and hardware. Decide on the length, width, and fullness.

MEASURE, MARK, AND CUT

Refer to your schematic and fill in the window treatment worksheets, page 104, adding seam allowance to the side and top edges, hem allowance to the bottom edge. Reverse the pieces to make pairs of curtains.

Ⓐ **PANEL** ✂cut 1 for each panel and 1 reversed for each lining, cutting as many whole and partial widths as needed.

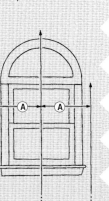

NOTE: The directions that follow are for making one lined panel. Repeat the directions for each panel you want to make. Before beginning, sew together whole and partial widths as needed.

TIPS FROM THE PROS

✂These curtains are easy to make but a little difficult to visualize. Before making your pattern and cutting the fabric, take the time to plan and mark the placement of the hooks—better yet, install them (refer to step 1). Mark the bottom of the arc/top of the side seam on the right side of each panel.

✂Many styles of decorative and plain hooks are available in drapery and hardware stores. Cabinet knobs are good alternatives.

✂Be sure your cord is compatible with the size of your hooks or knobs. Be sure also that your machine can stitch across the cord—or plan to attach the loops securely by hand.

✂For another look, insert fabric or ribbon ties instead of loops at the top edge, or make bias fabric loops and welting.

1 Determine the number of hooks needed, planning one at the top center of the arc, one on each side of the window at the bottom of the arc, and as many evenly spaced in between as desired.

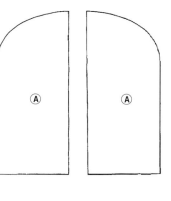

Use your imagination when selecting hardware for this design. For another look, use decorative drawer knobs instead of a custom metal rod with hooks.

2 Pin one end of a short piece of your cord (or whichever trim you are using) to a scrap of fabric. Loop the cord over a hook and pin the other end to fabric to form a loop of the desired size. Slip the loop off the hook and mark the cord where the pins secure it to the fabric. ▽

3 Unpin the loop, and measure the length between the marks; add 1" for seam allowance. Cut the required number of loops, cutting each to the length just calculated. If there is a flange, cut it off the cord.

4 Hem the lining and face fabric panels.

5 If you are using cording with a flange, sew it to the right side of the top edge of the face fabric panel (refer to Basics, page 115).

6 Count the spaces between the hook at the top and the hook at the bottom of the arc as planned in step 1. On the top edge of the panel, measure the seamline of the arc between the vertical edge seamlines and divide by the number of spaces to find the interval for the loops.

7 With the right sides together and cut edges aligned, pin the loops to the top edge of the panel; place one at the bottom of the arc, one adjacent to the leading-edge allowance, and space the others in between at the planned interval. Sew the loops to the panel on the seamline. ▽

TIPS FROM THE PROS

✄ If you've sewn cording to the face fabric panel, you'll probably find it easier to pin and sew the loops to the lining.

8 With the right sides together and all edges aligned, pin the panel to the lining. Sew together, leaving the bottom edges free. Trim the seam allowance from the ends of the arc, notch the curve, turn the panel right side out, and press.

Arch-top windows are generally challenging to dress. These loop-on panels allow the fabric to follow the top curve loosely—a great look that masks minor cutting errors.

9 If you did not sew cord to the top edge in step 5, sew your trim on now by hand.

10 Install the hooks if you have not already done so. Hang the curtain, placing the loops at the top of the center edges over the same hook.

11 Install purchased tiebacks or make and install coordinating ones from fabric and trim (refer to the Designer Detail on pages 38–39). If you wish, pin or tack the center edges of the curtains together a few inches below the top hook.

overlay tab curtains

ABOUT THE SAMPLE

These sheer tab curtains are made from two layers of cotton scrim. The top layer is narrower than the bottom layer; the hems create a band of deeper color along the edges. The panels hang from turned fabric tabs, and a facing on the back covers the upper seam allowance. To make a single-layer tab curtain, omit the directions for the overlay.

MATERIALS

Fabrics for curtain and overlay
Thread to match
Curtain rod or pole
Mounting hardware

PLANNING

Read Inside or Outside Mount?, page 94, then decide how your curtain will be mounted. Refer to Part Three, Basics, for information on measuring, calculating yardage, basic sewing techniques, and hardware. Read the tips preceding the directions, then decide on the length, width, and fullness of the panel and overlay, if any, and the number, length, and width of the tabs.

MEASURE, MARK, AND CUT

Fill in the window treatment worksheets, page 104. For sheer fabrics, do not piece the panels but make more panels to span your opening. Add hem allowances at the lower and side edges, seam allowance at the upper edge.

Ⓐ **PANEL** ✂cut 1 for each panel

Ⓑ **OVERLAY** ✂cut 1 for each panel

Ⓒ **TABS** ✂cut as many as needed, making them twice the finished width and adding seam allowances at the upper, lower, and side edges

Ⓓ **FACING** ✂cut 1 for each panel, 2¹/₂" deep and the same width as the panel

TIPS FROM THE PROS

✂Before filling in the window treatment worksheets, plan balanced repeating proportions for the hems, tabs, and spaces between tabs, adjusting the overall width as necessary—the exact fullness ratio isn't critical. For the sample, the hems are 3" deep, the tabs are 3" wide, and the space between the tabs is 6" wide; five tabs and four spaces make the panel 39" wide. Refer to step 4 to plan the tab spacing.

✂To find the width of the overlay, multiply the hem depth by 2 and subtract the result from the overall width of the bottom layer.

✂To determine the flat (unfolded) length of the tabs, loop a flexible measuring tape around your mounted pole and pinch the ends of the tape together at the desired distance below the pole. The flat length of the loop above your fingers is the finished (flat) length of the tab.

✂Measure the finished length of the panel downward from the lower edge of the tabs, not from the pole.

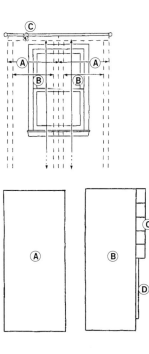

✂Sheer curtains will be prettiest if you do not piece the panel widths.

✂Refer to the Design Variations on page 45 for some other ways to prepare tabs.

NOTE: The directions that follow are for making one curtain with and without an overlay. Repeat the appropriate directions for each additional curtain you want to make. Before beginning, sew together whole and partial fabric widths as needed.

1 Referring to the Designer Detail on page 44, hem the lower and side edges of the panel (A) and overlay (B), making mitered corners.

2 Pin the overlay right side up to the right side of the panel between the side hems, aligning the upper edges; baste, then treat both layers as one. ▽

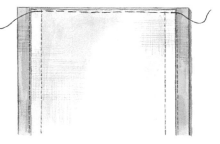

3 To make the tabs (C), fold each in half lengthwise with right sides together, aligning the cut edges, and stitch the lengthwise seam. Press the seam open, turn the tab right side out, center the seam on the back and press. Then fold each tab in half crosswise, aligning the cut edges; baste. ▷

✂To save time, cut one or two long strips for the tabs, sew and turn them, and then cut them to the appropriate length.

4 Place the curtain right side up on your worktable. Determine the positions of the tabs as follows, and then baste them in place.

✂To calculate the intervals between the tabs multiply the tab width by the number of tabs, then subtract the total from the finished (flat) curtain width. Divide the result by one less than the number of tabs to arrive at the distance between tabs.

✂Position one tab over each upper corner, aligning the side edges and the cut upper edges.

✂Measure the appropriate intervals along the upper edge of the panel between the outer tabs; mark with chalk or pins.

5 Press under ¹/₂" on the lower edge of the facing (D). Hem the side edges. Pin the facing, wrong side up, to the right side of the curtain, aligning the upper and side edges. Sew together along the cut edge through all thicknesses. ▽

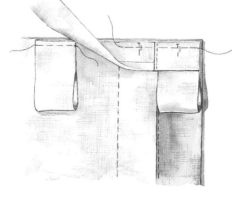

6 Fold the facing to the wrong side of the panel; the tabs will extend upward. Press. Pin all the layers together through the upper seam allowances. Edgestitch the lower fold of the facing. Hand stitch the side edges of the facing to the panel. △

Layered sheer panels in graduated sizes and contrasting colors give a simple elegance to basic tab curtains.

TIPS FROM THE PROS

✂If you are making a single-layer curtain, you can topstitch the tabs to the top. When cutting, add an upper hem allowance to the panel, add 2" to the length of each tab, and omit the facing. Hem the upper edge of the curtain. Instead of basting the tab ends together, fold the cut ends under ¹/₂" before folding each tab in half crosswise, then sandwich the upper edge of the panel between the tab ends, overlapping by 1", and topstitch.

7 Slide the tabs onto the pole.

sheer mitered hems

Mitered corner seams make topstitched sheer hems bulk-free and neat. The miters are not difficult to sew, but keeping the top and bottom folds of the hem perfectly straight and parallel can be challenging. Pressing them over a template assures crisp perfection. The width of the template should equal the finished hem depth (3" for this project); make the template as long as convenient. Tagboard is the ideal template material: manila folders offer an easy source.

TIPS FROM THE PROS

✄For best results, use a straightedge and craft knife or rotary cutter when cutting your template.

✄This technique can be used on heavier fabrics, but professionals usually use the method given on page 114 in order to preserve the excess panel length.

1 Cut a 3"-wide template. Draw a line parallel to and 1/2" from one long edge. ▽

2 Place the piece to be hemmed wrong side up on your ironing board. Place the template on it with the edge with the drawn line closest to the cut edge of the fabric. Fold the cut edge of the fabric over the template, aligning it with the drawn line, and press the fold to form a crease. Reposition the template and repeat until 1/2" has been pressed up on all hem edges. ▽

3 With the template inside the crease, fold the fabric and the template to the wrong side. Press the new fold to form a second crease parallel to the first. Reposition the template and repeat until this additional 3" has been pressed up on all hem edges. Unfold, revealing the creaselines.

A neatly mitered hem is especially effective on sheer fabrics where the shadow of every seam embellishes the border.

4 Keep the fabric wrong side up. Using a small 45-degree right-angle triangle, mark a diagonal line across each corner at the intersection of the inner creaselines. ▽

5 At each corner, fold the fabric diagonally, wrong side out, aligning the adjacent cut edges (fold along the dash line in the drawing above). Pin together on the line drawn in the step 4, and sew between the inner and outer creases only. Trim the excess fabric at the point. ▽

6 Press the mitered seams open, re-pressing the first creaseline as you do so. Turn the hem right side out, push out the points, and press each corner flat. Pin, baste if necessary, and edgestitch along the inner crease.

tab **alternatives**

While your fabric choice will influence the formality of tab curtains, you can also alter their demeanor with different styles of tabs.

TIES

Instead of sewing closed loops to the top of the curtain, sew on ties. Don't make the ties too wide since they would be awkward. Tie them over the rod in knots or bows as you wish.

You can topstitch the midpoint of one long tie at each interval, or use two shorter pieces. For two pieces, insert the tie ends between the panel and a facing or lining, or finish the ends and topstitch in place. To create the tassel-like knot shown here, make one tie of each pair longer than its mate, and then tie them in front of the curtain pole. ▽

BUTTON TABS

For a tailored look, button one end of the tab to the front of the curtain. Plan the tab length in the usual way, but curve or point the front end, adding an overlap allowance equal to somewhat more than the button diameter; also add a seam allowance to the back end. Bind all edges but the back end. Make the buttonhole. With the cut edges aligned, place the wrong side of each tab against the right side of the curtain, then align the facing right side against the tabs, sew across the top seamline, and fold the facing to the wrong side. Sew a button to the curtain opposite each folded-down tab. ▽

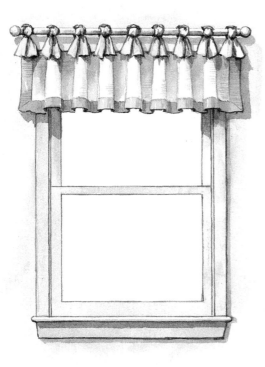

simple
sash curtains

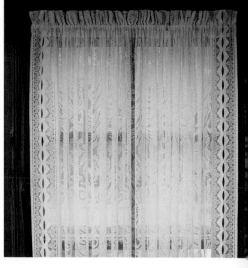

ABOUT THE SAMPLE

These curtains were made from polyester-blend lace with a woven-in border along each selvage. There is a small heading at the top and bottom of each panel. For an hourglass variation, see the Design Variation on page 48.

MATERIALS

Fabric

Thread to match

Curtain rods

Mounting hardware

PLANNING

Read Rod Pockets and Headings, page 32. Refer to Part Three, Basics, for information on measuring, calculating yardage, basic sewing techniques, and hardware. Decide how your curtain will be mounted. Decide on the length, width, and fullness, and the rod-pocket and heading depths. If using a sheer fabric, refer to Basics, page 112, and decide on a finishing method for the side edges.

MEASURE, MARK, AND CUT

Fill in the window treatment worksheet, page 104. If your fabric has decorative selvages and your panel will use the full fabric width, you can omit side hem allowances.

(A) **PANEL** ✂ **cut as many whole and partial widths as needed for each panel**

TIPS FROM THE PROS

✂ Keep your measuring diagram handy so you can quickly mark the rod-pocket and heading allowances.

✂ You can hide the rod in a lace or sheer pocket by doubling the depth of the top allowance, pressing down the doubled allowance, then folding, pressing, and topstitching as usual the hem and heading, if any. Slip the rod into the pocket between the back two layers of fabric.

NOTE: The directions that follow are for making one curtain panel. Repeat the directions for each additional panel you want to make. Before beginning, sew together whole and partial fabric widths as needed.

1 Hem the side edges of the panel (A).

✂ If using a lace or sheer fabric consider finishing the side edges with a rolled hem or stitch-turn-stitch baby hem (refer to Basics, page 113).

✂ If desired, add trim at or parallel to the side edges at this time.

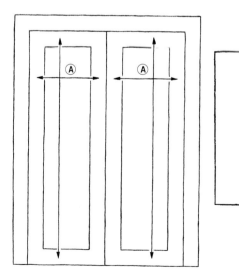

Each sash panel uses the full width of the lace and takes advantage of the beading (eyelet pattern) at the selvage. The heading gives a crisp finish, but is optional.

TIPS FROM THE PROS

✂ Use a gentle marking method for lace and other sheers. Try using quilter's masking tape to mark straight lines, removing it as soon as you are done with it. Tailor's chalk and nonpermanent ink fabric markers are also good choices for delicate fabrics.

✂ Before using pins on sheers, test on a scrap to be sure they won't permanently mar the fabric.

2 Add together your rod-pocket depth, your heading depth, and the $^3/_4$" hem allowance and stitching margin. On the front of the panel, mark a line this distance below and parallel to the top edge. Mark a line the same distance above and parallel to the lower edge (refer to the Designer Detail on page 32).

3 Fold ¹/₂" to the wrong side along the upper edge of the panel and press. Fold the fabric to the wrong side again along the marked line and press. Topstitch through all layers along the first fold. Measure, mark, and topstitch the heading. Repeat on the lower edge of the panel. ▽

4 Slip the rods through the pockets, gathering the fabric evenly. Mount the upper rod, then the bottom rod so that the curtain is taut.

Lace sash curtains are a classic touch for French doors. The puddling scarf swag is a fitting finish for this tall stairwell; to make it, adapt the loop-tie swag on page 65.

hourglass sash curtains

An hourglass curtain appears to get its silhouette from a tie, but the panel must be specially shaped or the tie will cause the top and bottom edges of the panel to slide toward the middle of the rods.

TIPS FROM THE PROS

✄ Because the rod pocket and any heading must be folded along an inside curve, keep them as shallow as possible.

1 To begin, plan and cut a panel as you would for a regular sash curtain, but add 10" to the overall length for a shaping allowance. Hem the side edges of the panel.

2 Press the panel in half lengthwise and then crosswise, unfold it and lay it face up on a large work surface. Working from the crosswise fold toward one end, measure a distance equal to half the finished length of the curtain and mark a line across the panel with tailor's chalk. Measure and mark the same distance from the crosswise fold toward the other end. ▷

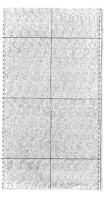

TIPS FROM THE PROS

✄ To avoid confusion later, mark the first pair of lines with one color chalk and subsequent lines with a second color.

3 With the panel still on the worktable, finger-gather the panel along its entire length to its finished width. Then draw it into an hourglass shape and tie string temporarily around the center, at the crosswise fold; the panel ends and marked lines should now curve outward. Adjust the fanned ends so that the width across each marked line is equal to the finished curtain width.

TIPS FROM THE PROS

✄ Weight the corners of the arranged panel to maintain the shape while you finish marking.

4 Measuring from the crosswise fold as before, mark two straight lines across the gathered panel. The center of each new line should align with the center of the previous line, the ends should be closer to the panel ends. ▷

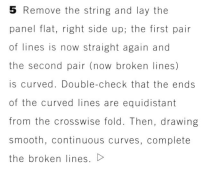

5 Remove the string and lay the panel flat, right side up; the first pair of lines is now straight again and the second pair (now broken lines) is curved. Double-check that the ends of the curved lines are equidistant from the crosswise fold. Then, drawing smooth, continuous curves, complete the broken lines. ▷

6 Brush away the straight lines. Parallel to each curved line and closer to the panel ends, mark the rod-pocket (and any heading) allowance. Mark the hem allowance and stitching margin ³/₄" outside this line. Cut on the last (outermost) curved lines. ▷

TIPS FROM THE PROS

✄ You can cut identical symmetrical curves by drawing the curve halfway across one end of the panel, refolding the panel in quarters, and then cutting through all layers on the marked curve.

7 Press out the creased folds, then fold and stitch the rod pockets and headings, if any, at the upper and lower edges. Brush away the markings. ▷

8 Slip the rods through the pockets, then mount the curtain on the sash so that the vertical center is taut. Pull the curtain into an hourglass shape at the center and tie with string or scrap fabric.

9 Make a straight tie (refer to Basics, page 118), wrap it around the curtain, and tie it in a simple bow or knot. Tack or pin it to the curtain if necessary. ▷

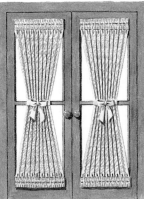

rolled stagecoach valance

TIPS FROM THE PROS

- This valance works best on a narrow window—a wide panel would be cumbersome to roll and any seams would be visible.
- Use an inside mount to leave as small a gap as possible between the valance and window.
- Alternatively, this valance can be mounted on a rod. To do this, you will need to make a rod pocket on the top.
- If you'd prefer a roll-up shade that can be raised and lowered, consider making the Easy Roll-Up Shade, pages 90–91.
- The wrong side of the valance will show on the front of the roll. Consider using a woven fabric that looks the same on both sides.

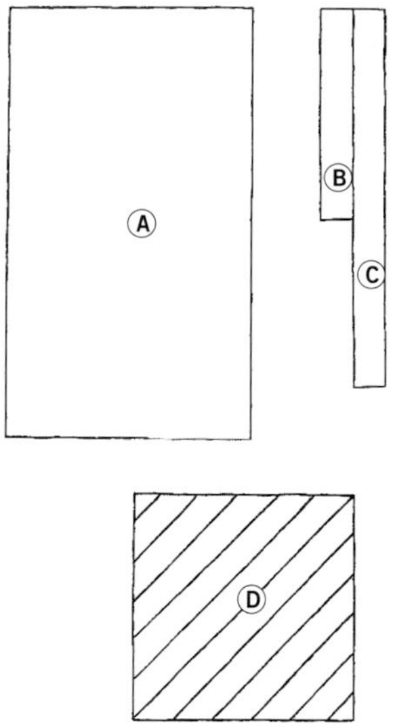

Stagecoach valances are tailored yet perky. The fabric should be crisp, but not stiff, to give a good roll. In a hurry? You can even use heavy paper for this design.

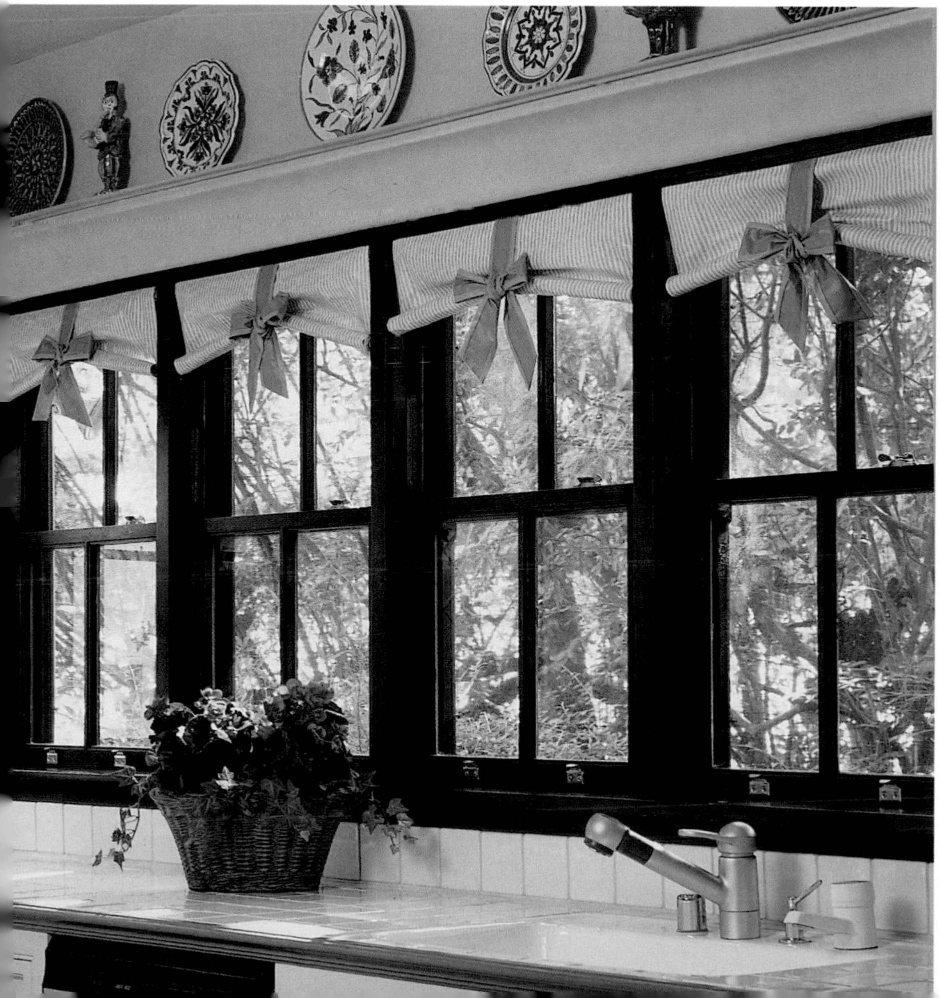

ABOUT THE SAMPLE

This striped cotton valance is a snap to make; the cut edges are sealed with a liquid fray retardant. The valance is held up at the center by a carrier with an attached bow; a $^{1}/_{2}$"-deep binding finishes the edges of the carrier and bow. The valance and carrier are attached to a mounting board.

MATERIALS

Fabrics for curtain, carrier/bow, and binding
Thread to match
Mounting board and hardware

PLANNING

Read Inside or Outside Mount?, page 94, referring to the information on Roman shades, then read Mounting Boards, page 108. Read step 1 to plan and measure, and make a schematic diagram for your valance. Read step 3 to plan the carrier and bow. Refer to Part Three, Basics, for information on calculating yardage and basic sewing techniques.

MEASURE, MARK, AND CUT

Refer to your schematic and fill in the window treatment worksheets, page 104, including allowances on the valance as planned. Cut the strips for the carrier and bow to whatever finished width you desire.

- Ⓐ **VALANCE** ✂**cut 1**
- Ⓑ **CARRIER** ✂**cut 1**
- Ⓒ **BOW** ✂**cut 1**
- Ⓓ **BIAS STRIPS** ✂**cut 2" wide, enough to trim the side edges of the carrier and bow**

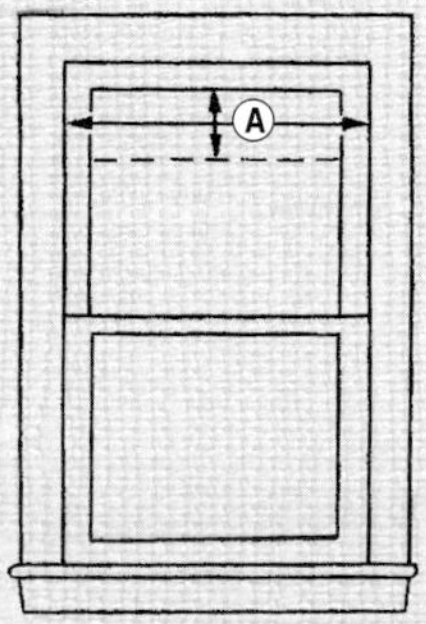

rolled stagecoach valance

1 Plan and measure for your valance (A). Note each measurement on your schematic.

✄ Determine the finished width of the valance.

✄ Decide the finished depth of the valance (when rolled).

✄ Determine the size of the roll at the lower edge of the valance before you buy your fabric: Roll up one end of the fabric to judge the effect. Mark the bottom of the roll with a pin, then unroll the fabric and measure the length that was rolled. This measurement is the roll allowance.

✄ Add an attachment allowance at the top to staple to the mounting board. ▽

TIPS FROM THE PROS

✄ If you plan to mount your valance on a rod, omit the mounting allowance and add a rod-pocket allowance (refer to Rod Pockets and Headings, page 32).

✄ If you want to hem the lower or side edges, add appropriate allowances. The lower hem will be concealed inside the roll, but the side hems will show on the front when the valance is rolled up.

✄ If you prefer to line the valance, make the lining flush with the edges of the face fabric—add seam allowance to the lower and side edges.

2 Cut out the valance. If desired, finish the top edge.

✄ If you have not added side and bottom hem allowances, seal the side and lower edges with liquid fray retardant.

✄ If you have added side and bottom hem allowances, fold and stitch the hems (refer to Basics, page 113).

3 The best way to judge the proportions of the carrier (B) and bow (C) is to make a muslin mock-up. Place your valance on your worktable and roll up the lower edge as planned. Cut a strip of muslin 2"–4" wide and, aligning the top edges, place it under the valance. Wrap it up, over the roll, and back up the front of the valance to the top edge. △

4 Cut another strip, tie it in a bow, and place it on the carrier over the roll. Cut the tails of the bow on an angle. Adjust the proportions if necessary.

5 Undo the muslin mock-up and, from the appropriate fabric, cut strips of the desired width and long enough to make the carrier and the bow.

TIPS FROM THE PROS

✄ To save time, cut one long strip for the carrier and bow. Complete the next step, and then cut the strip into segments of the proper length.

6 Using the bias strips (D), bind the edges of the carrier/bow strips (refer to Basics, page 116).

7 If you've not yet done so, measure and cut from the bound strips an appropriate length for the carrier. Measure and cut another strip for the bow. Seal the cut ends of both strips with a liquid fray retardant. To create the points, fold under each end of the tail on an angle and tack in place.

8 Use tailor's chalk to mark the mounting allowance on the right and wrong sides of both ends of the carrier. Measure and mark the midpoint of each line. Also mark a point halfway between the ends of the mounting board.

9 Place the mounting board on your worktable. Center one end of the carrier, wrong side up, on the top of the board; align the marked allowance with the top front edge of the board. Staple in place. ▽

10 On the right side of the top edge of the valance, mark the mounting allowance. With the valance right side up, place the mounting allowance on the top face of the mounting board; align the marked allowance with the top front edge of the board. Staple in place.

✄ For a rod-pocket valance, center the carrier, right side up, on the top edge of the right side of the valance; sew it into the rod-pocket allowance. Then roll up the valance as before, wrap the carrier to the wrong side, and pin it to the back of the rod pocket. Adjust the tension after you've mounted the valance.

Bound edges give these bows a tailored look—bias stripes could be fun here. You can alternatively make plain ties or use ribbon—the wired-edge variety ties nicely.

11 With the board and valance still on your table, roll up the valance as before; pin the roll in place on the wrong side. Fold the carrier up and over the roll and valance, then staple the mounting allowance to the top face of the board. ▽

12 Install the board. Remove the pins from the roll and adjust so it hangs taut and centered in the carrier.

13 Tie the bow. Pin or tack the bow to the carrier on the front of the rolled portion of the valance.

TIPS FROM THE PROS

✂If you have trouble tying a nice bow, try this trick: Form the fabric strip into a loop with tails and sew the tails together as shown. Then pinch the center by wrapping with thread. For a knot, wrap the center with a short fabric strip. ▽

tailed stagecoach valance

design variations

If you use two carriers instead of one, and gently pleat, rather than roll, the bottom edge, the center portion of the valance will drape in a small swag, the sides in small tails.

You can use ribbon instead of fabric for the carriers; for a feminine or informal look (the effect will depend upon your fabric and ribbon choice), make the tails of the bows extra-long. Or, for a more tailored look, omit the bows. To add more punch, make each carrier in two pieces and button them together; if you use more than one button (or buttonhole) the carrier will be adjustable. You can bind all but the top edges, or make simple turned ties.

graceful tapered valance

ABOUT THE SAMPLE

This informal cotton print valance has a simply curved hemline that tapers into tails. The sample is self-lined; use a contrasting fabric for the lining if desired.

MATERIALS

Fabric(s) for valance and lining
Thread to match
Curtain rod or pole
Mounting hardware

PLANNING

Read Inside or Outside Mount?, page 94, and Measuring for a Rod Pocket, page 99. Refer to Part Three, Basics, for information on measuring, calculating yardage, basic sewing techniques, and hardware. Decide how your valance will be mounted. Decide on the length and width of the valance center and tails, the fullness, and the rod-pocket depth.

MEASURE, MARK, AND CUT

Fill in the window treatment worksheets, page 104. Refer to steps 1 and 2 to mark and cut out the fabric pieces.

Ⓐ **VALANCE** ✂ **cut 1 for each valance and 1 for each lining**

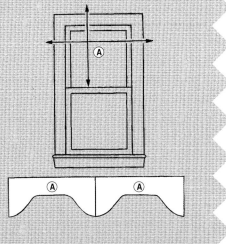

TIPS FROM THE PROS

✂ Divide the total valance width by 3 to arrive at the width of the center and each tail, or use proportions appropriate for your design.

✂ If you are unsure of the proportions that will be best for the lower edge of this project, read Arched Curtains, page 101, to see how to make a test pattern.

✂ To add a heading, refer to the Designer Detail on page 32.

✂ Keep your measuring diagram handy so you can quickly mark the valance shape and the rod-pocket and any heading allowances.

✂ You may save on fabric if you cut a tapered valance as two shaped tails and a rectangular center that you sew together before beginning.

NOTE: The directions that follow are for making one lined valance. Repeat the directions for each additional valance you want to make. Before beginning, sew together whole and partial fabric widths as needed.

1 Fold your fabric in half lengthwise and mark half the valance (A) onto it:

✂ At a distance from the top edge equal to at least 2 times the top allowance of the valance, draw a line perpendicular to the fold and extending from it a distance equal to the valance width. This line is the bottom of the rod pocket.

✂ Draw a line perpendicular to the first one and extending downward from it a distance equal to the valance length. This line is the side edge of the valance.

The lining does show on a tapered valance, so use a contrasting fabric if you like. You can also insert a trim in the bottom seam—ball or tassel fringes can be great fun.

✂ Mark a dot on the first line at a distance from the fold equal to half the width of the valance center. Mark another dot below the first one at a distance equal to the depth of the valance center. Draw a perpendicular line from the fold to the lower dot, and then extend the line in a gentle curve to the lower end of the vertical (side edge) line. Extend the shape upward a distance equal to the rod-pocket allowance plus the heading allowance, if any, plus $^3/_4$" for hem allowance and stitching margin ▽

2 Add seam allowance to the lower and side edges. The outermost marked lines are the cutting lines. △

TIPS FROM THE PROS

✂If you plan to make several valances, you may prefer to make a paper pattern and use it to cut out all the fabric pieces at the same time.

3 Cut out the valance, then use it as a pattern to cut out the lining.

4 With the right sides together and cut edges aligned, pin the lining to the valance. Sew the pieces together along the side and lower edges. Trim the corners diagonally and, if necessary, clip or notch the curved seam allowance. Turn the valance right side out; press. Baste the layers together $1/2$" (the hem turn-in allowance) inside the open (top) edge. ▽

5 Add together your rod-pocket depth, any heading depth, and the $3/4$" hem and stitching margin. On the front of the valance, mark a chalk line this distance below and parallel to the top edge (refer to the Designer Detail on page 32).

6 Fold the upper edge of the valance to the back along the basting line and press. Fold to the back again along the chalk line and press. Topstitch through all layers along the first fold. Measure, mark, and topstitch any heading. ▽

7 Slip the rod through the pocket, gathering the fabric evenly. Mount the valance.

TIPS FROM THE PROS

✂You can reduce bulk in the pocket and heading by trimming away the lining from the pocket, heading, and turn-in allowances. If you do so, be sure to hem the open ends of the pocket and heading.

The tails of paired tapered valances add vertical lines to a wide window. In this small breakfast nook they're soft yet fuss-free; traditional blinds assure privacy.

classic **sunburst curtain**

ABOUT THE SAMPLE

This inside-mounted curtain was made from a plain, lightweight sheer. The pocket on the top edge slides over a flexible plastic rod; the lower edge is gathered and tacked into a rosette. If you prefer, you can make a drawstring casing on the lower edge and cover it with a separate rosette (refer to the Designer Detail on page 58).

MATERIALS

Fabric
Thread to match
Flexible curtain rod with appropriate cup hooks and sockets for mounting

PLANNING

Read all of the project directions before beginning. Refer to steps 1–4 to plan, measure, and calculate yardage. Refer to Part Three, Basics, for information about basic sewing techniques and hardware.

MEASURE, MARK, AND CUT

Fill in the window treatment worksheets, page 104.

Ⓐ **PANEL** ✂cut as many whole and partial widths as needed

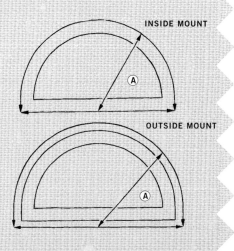

INSIDE MOUNT

OUTSIDE MOUNT

✂Because there is so much bulk at the center of a sunburst curtain, lightweight fabrics and a fullness ratio no greater than 2:1 are a must for this design.
✂A sunburst curtain relies on equal tension from the center out to the curve—you'll get the best results on semicircular windows.
✂You can use a sunburst curtain on an elliptical window if the difference between the window's height and its radius at the base is no more than 6".
✂If your window's radius is greater than 36", the amount of fabric at the center of a sunburst curtain will be unwieldy and unattractive—don't use this design.

1 Plan your curtain. Make a sketch of the window and a schematic diagram so you can visualize the project.
✂Decide how to mount the curtain (refer to Inside or Outside Mount?, pages 94–95).
✂Decide on the length, width, fullness, rod-pocket depth, and the heading depth, if any. Decide on the rosette diameter.

2 Measure for your curtain, referring to the diagrams at left. For an inside mount, measure inside the perimeter of the sash. For an outside mount, measure at the curve where you will mount the hardware, then measure the base between the lower ends of the curve. Write all the dimensions on your sketch.

Ⓐ

3 Determine the cutting dimensions, filling in the worksheets as you go.
✂To find the cut length, divide the window base by 2, then add to that number the desired rosette diameter; enter the total in the panel length column of the length worksheet. Add the top allowance (the rod-pocket allowance plus the heading allowance, if any, plus $3/4$" for the hem turn-in allowance and stitching margin); refer to Measuring for a Rod Pocket, page 99.
✂To find the cut width, measure the perimeter curve and multiply that number by the fullness ratio appropriate for your design. Add allowances for narrow side hems.

TIPS FROM THE PROS

✂Don't get confused—on a sunburst curtain the length (the radius) is shorter than the width.
✂If your window is semicircular, you can easily calculate the perimeter curve mathematically. Multiply the base by 3.1415 and divide the result by 2.
✂If using a sheer fabric, refer to Basics, page 112, and decide on a narrow finishing method for the side edges.

The radiating folds of a sunburst curtain are especially apparent in a plain sheer fabric.

A sunburst curtain sits comfortably above a soft-fold Roman shade in this contemporary bedroom. Honey-colored translucent fabrics emphasize the soft, serene effect. The directions for the shade begin on page 76.

4 Calculate the yardage:

✄For fabric that runs vertically, divide the cut width by the usable fabric width to determine the number of widths needed. Then multiply the cut length by the number of widths and divide by 36 for the number of yards.

✄If railroading fabric (cutting the length on the crosswise grain), divide the cut width by 36 for the number of yards.

5 Cut out the panel (A). Sew together whole and partial widths as needed.

TIPS FROM THE PROS

✄Use a gentle marking method for lace and other sheers. Try using quilter's masking tape to mark straight lines, removing it as soon as you are done with it. Tailor's chalk and nonpermanent ink fabric markers are also good choices for delicate fabrics.

✄Before using pins on sheers, test on a scrap to be sure they won't permanently mar the fabric.

6 Fold and stitch narrow side hems on the panel.

7 Add together your rod-pocket depth, your heading depth, if any, and the $^3/_4$" hem allowance and stitching margin. On the front of the panel, mark a line this distance below and parallel to the top edge (refer to the Designer Detail on page 32).

8 Fold $^1/_2$" to the wrong side along the upper edge of the panel and press. Fold the fabric to the wrong side again along the marked line and press. Topstitch through all layers along the first fold. Measure, mark, and topstitch the heading, if any. ▽

9 Slip the rod through the pocket, gathering the fabric evenly. Install the rod over the window in the supporting cup hooks and sockets. If necessary, slit the back of the rod pocket to accommodate each cup hook; seal the cut edges with liquid fray retardant.

10 Pull together the loose lower edge of the curtain at the center and wrap tightly with a rubber band, round elastic, or string. Adjust the tension and gathers evenly. ▽

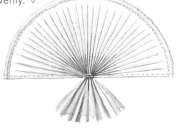

11 Tuck under the excess fabric, arranging the folds and tacking the edge behind the rosette; arrange and tack until the fabric is secure and you are satisfied with the rosette's appearance.

TIPS FROM THE PROS

✄Experiment with the rosette. You may want to trim some of the extra length.

✄Don't worry about the unfinished lower edge—you can finish it before you launder the curtain for the first time.

✄You can secure the curtain center to a wooden window with a cup hook, pushpin, or thumbtack hidden inside the folds of the rosette.

reversible
cuffed curtain

ABOUT THE SAMPLE

You can make this reversible curtain for a bathtub, as shown, or for a window or door. The sample is made from complementary woven cottons. It has a 16"-deep foldover cuff resembling a valance. On both the face fabric and lining, 1"-wide grosgrain ribbon is stitched to the cuff foldline, and gaps in the topstitching create loops through which 18"-long ribbon ties are inserted. If you don't wish the curtain to be reversible, sew ribbon to the lining only.

MATERIALS

Fabrics for curtain and lining
Ribbon
Thread to match
Curtain rod or pole
Mounting hardware

PLANNING

Refer to Part Three, Basics, for information on measuring, calculating yardage, basic sewing techniques, and hardware. Read the tips preceding the project directions, then decide on the finished length and width, the depth of the cuff, and the fullness, if any.

MEASURE, MARK, AND CUT

Fill in the window treatment worksheets, page 104.

(A) **PANEL** ✂cut 1 for each panel and 1 for each lining, cutting as many whole and partial widths as needed.

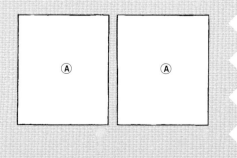

TIPS FROM THE PROS

✂Measure your shower curtain liner and use those dimensions as the starting point for planning the length and width of your curtain. Add length at the top for the cuff; add length at the bottom to extend the panel to the floor if you wish.

✂To make a window panel, measure as for tab curtains (refer to Basics, page 96) and add the desired depth of the cuff to the length measurement.

✂Do your ribbon math. Use a scrap to estimate the length needed for the ties—this curtain required about 10 yards total.

✂Nondirectional patterns such as stripes, checks, plaids, and dots work best on this project because the lining is inverted on the front of the cuff.

✂Consider cutting the lower edge of the cuff (the top edge of the curtain) in a scallop or zigzag, or edging it with trim.

NOTE: The directions that follow are for making one lined panel. Repeat the directions for each panel you want to make. Before beginning, sew together whole and partial widths as needed.

1 Cut a length of ribbon to fit the width of the lining (A), including seam allowance. Cut a second length for the face fabric. Mark the midpoint of each length with a pin, also mark the side seam allowances.

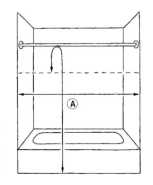

Companion patterns with common colors are good choices for cuffed curtains.

TIPS FROM THE PROS

✂Plastic shower curtain liners are not always symmetrical, so cut the ribbon a little longer than necessary, and, when you mark it in the next step, be sure to work from the midpoint out and note which end of the ribbon will be at which edge of the plastic liner. (The right side of the lining will face the plastic liner.)

2 Mark the locations of the hanging spaces on the ribbon to correspond to the grommets on your plastic liner. (For a window curtain, mark at the intervals desired.)

✂Measure the distance from center to center between two adjacent grommets, and, with tailor's chalk, mark at this interval along the ribbon.

✂Measure on both sides of each chalk mark a distance equal to half the ribbon width plus a 1/8" allowance for ease; mark with vertical lines between the long edges of the ribbon using a second color of tailor's chalk.

✂Connect the endpoints of the widely spaced pairs of marked lines to form rectangles, leaving gaps between (opposite each grommet) where the ribbon will be inserted. Draw a partial rectangle between the last marked line on each end and the pin at the seamline. ▽

[ribbon diagram image]

3 Spread the lining on your worktable right side up with the upper cut edge toward you. Measure up from the cut edge a distance equal to the depth of the cuff plus the upper seam allowance plus the width of the ribbon; mark with chalk or pins, then mark the midpoint of the line.

4 Using the marked line as a guide, pin and baste the ribbon to the cuff portion of the lining; be sure the midpoints match. Pin and baste the second ribbon to the face panel in the same way. ▽

TIPS FROM THE PROS

✄Before basting, check that the ribbon is oriented to align with the grommets. Measure in from each end to see if the spaces correspond to the end grommets.

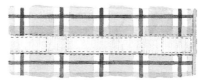

5 Sew on the ribbons as basted. Start at the center of the ribbon and, working toward each end, topstitch the marked edges of the whole and partial rectangles; backstitch the short edges of each to secure, and cut the threads between rectangles. The gaps between the topstitched rectangles are the hanging loops. Remove the basting. △

6 With the right sides together and cut edges aligned, pin the lining to the face panel. Sew the pieces together, leaving an opening in the lower edge for turning. Trim the corners. Turn the curtain right side out; press. Press the seam allowances to the inside at the opening and slipstitch the opening closed.

7 Place the curtain, lining side up, on your worktable and smooth out the fabric layers. Pin the layers together about 1" above and below the ribbon. Topstitch the lining and face fabric together just outside the ribbon edges. Do not catch the ribbon with the stitches.

8 Cut the required number of ribbon ties. Seal the cut ends with liquid fray retardant. Slide a tie under the topstitched ribbon at each gap in the stitching. ▽

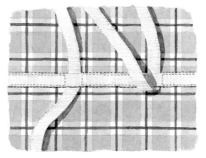

9 Install the curtain rod if you are not using an existing one. Fold the cuff to the front of the curtain. Hang the curtain by passing the lining end of each ribbon through the corresponding grommet on the plastic liner and then looping the ribbon ties around the rod and tying them into bows.

A cuffed curtain is as appropriate at a window as it is at a shower. For a different look, use one layer of a reversible sheer.

special bows and rosettes

When you want to give a window treatment an extra-special finish, make a separate bow or rosette that you sew or pin in place. These sculptural embellishments don't "just happen"—they're carefully planned and constructed. But they're not difficult to make and nothing outdoes them for customizing a design.

MALTESE CROSS

A Maltese cross is a double bow without tails. Depending upon your fabric choice it will look elegant, tailored, or jaunty. Begin with strips of fabric or ribbon in a width that is a little less than half the diameter desired for the cross (for example, for a 4"-diameter cross, begin with $1^{1}/_{2}$"-wide ribbon). If using fabric, finish or bind the long edges before beginning. You'll need a covered or decorative button for the center. ▽

1 Cut two lengths of fabric or ribbon, each a little longer than twice the desired diameter of the cross. Sew the ends of each strip together to make two rings.

2 Flatten the rings into loops, centering the seam between the folded ends. By hand, sew gathers across the center of each layer of one loop. Hand gather the center of the second loop through both layers at once. ▽

3 Slip the first loop inside the second one at right angles and stitch together at the center. Sew the covered button over the gathers on the side without the joining seam.

Don't shy away from rosettes—used quietly they're not at all pretentious. In fact, they offer an easy way to add a subtle flourish to an understated design. Of course, if your design is grand you can go to town with one of these. Use scrim, washed muslin, organza, taffeta—whatever suits.

CHOUX ROSETTE

Choux rosettes take a lot of tiny hand stitches, but they're worth the effort. Make the puckered puff tight and controlled or loose and flamboyant, as you wish. You'll need a scrap of buckram or other stiff material for the base. ▽

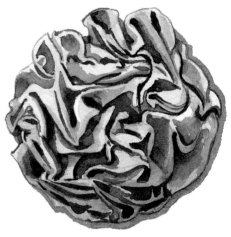

1 From the buckram, cut a circle with a diameter about half that desired for the finished rosette. From the rosette fabric, cut a circle with a diameter three times that of the buckram.

2 Gather the perimeter of the fabric circle to fit the perimeter of the buckram circle. Pin the edges together, right sides out. Overcast the edge by hand or machine.

3 Flatten the fabric pouf so that the buckram is centered under it, and pin the centers together. By hand, tack the centers together with a single stitch; do not break the thread. ▽

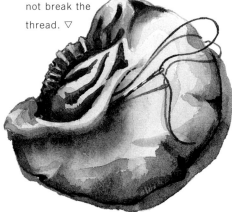

4 To create the puckered center, push a bit of the loose fabric toward the center and take another stitch. Continue to arrange and stitch the fabric until you've sewn a rosette of the desired tightness.

RUFFLE ROSETTE

These rosettes are easier to make than choux. You can use a strip of fabric or a piece of ribbon—it should be a little wider than the radius of the desired rosette, and 1½–2 times as long as the circumference (20" is the maximum length). If using fabric, make a tube or finish or bind the long edges before beginning. ▷

1 Placing the stitches ½"–1 " from the edge, gather one long edge of the strip. Then sew the ends of the strip together to make a ring.

2 Adjust the gathers to pull up the center of the ring as tightly as possible. Hold the ring by the gathers, pinching the center together between your fingers, and hand stitch straight through the gathers several times, rotating between stitches; secure the thread. △

3 Turn the rosette over so the ruffled center faces down. Steam the longer ruffle so it fans out. If it doesn't hold a nice shape, smooth the longer part over the central ruffle and bind with an elastic band. Let the rosette sit overnight, then remove the elastic.

TIPS FROM THE PROS

✄For a variation of this technique, make the ruffle strip wider and longer and place the gathers halfway between the long edges. Pouf, fold, and tack the fullness as necessary after gathering and pulling the center together. Experiment to find pleasing proportions.

✄Here's another way to make a ruffled rosette: Prepare a 3" x 60" ruffle, tapering the gathering stitches diagonally across one end. Cut a circle of buckram about 3" in diameter. Beginning with the square end of the ruffle at the perimeter of the buckram, wrap and hand stitch the ruffle to the buckram in a tight spiral. ▽

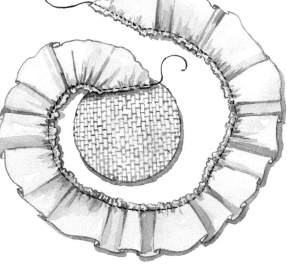

scalloped valance

ABOUT THE SAMPLE

This scalloped valance is one wide panel pleated to the width of the mounting board. Made from a cotton print, it is self-lined and a narrow welting firms the lower edge and helps to round out the pleats. If you wish to make coordinating curtains, refer to Basic Rod-Pocket Panels, pages 30–33.

MATERIALS

Fabric for valance and lining
Cable cording
Thread to match
Hook-and-loop tape (optional)
Mounting board and hardware

PLANNING

Read Inside or Outside Mount?, page 94, and Mounting Boards, page 108, then decide how your valance will be mounted. Refer to steps 1–3 of the project directions to plan your valance. Refer to Part Three, Basics, for information on measuring, calculating yardage, basic sewing techniques, and hardware.

MEASURE, MARK, AND CUT

Fill in the window treatment worksheets, page 104. Cut the valance and lining as rectangles, cut the scalloped edge later.

Ⓐ **VALANCE** ✂cut 1 for valance and 1 for lining, cutting as many whole and partial widths as needed

Ⓑ **BIAS STRIPS** ✂cut 1¹/₂" wide, enough to trim the lower and side edges of the valance

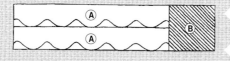

1 To determine the scallop width, first decide how many scallops you'd like across the valance; an odd number will look best. The width of the pleated valance must be equal to a multiple of the scallop width plus half the volume of one pleat. This will allow for the quarter-pleat return under the pleat at each end of the valance. ▽

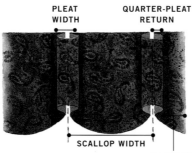

PLEAT WIDTH   QUARTER-PLEAT RETURN

SCALLOP WIDTH

BOARD END RETURN

To find the width of the scallops:
✂Determine the finished width of the pleated valance, excluding any end returns. (This is equal to the length of the mounting board.)
✂Determine the volume of one pleat (twice the width of the pleat showing on the right side of the valance).
✂Divide the volume of one pleat by 2 and subtract the result from the length of the mounting board. Divide the remainder by the desired number of scallops.

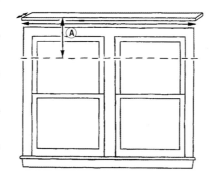

2 To determine cutting dimensions, first calculate the unpleated width of the valance: Multiply the number of scallops by the scallop width; also multiply the number of pleats by the volume of one pleat. Add the resulting numbers together. To this figure add half the volume of one pleat. Enter this sum in the panel width column of the width worksheet. Complete the two worksheets in the usual manner.

TIPS FROM THE PROS

✂To judge the effect, mock up a portion of the valance; use fabric similar in weight to your final lined valance.
✂The finished pleated valance must be at least as wide as your window. If you're using an outside mount, base your math on the desired finished width; if this results in a scallop width with an awkward fraction, round it up to the next workable increment, multiply by the number of scallops, and add half the volume of one pleat. Use the total as the pleated valance width/mounting board length.

3 Referring to the diagram, opposite below, make a pattern for the scallop and pleat repeat; label it as shown:
✂Draw a rectangle: Make the width equal to 1¹/₂ scallop widths plus the volume of one pleat; make the depth equal to the greatest depth of the valance.
✂Measure and mark the width of the scallop at the right end of the rectangle and of a half-scallop at the left end. The space in between should equal the volume of one pleat.

✄Determine the shortest depth of the scallop, which will fall at the midpoint of each pleat. Mark a line this distance below and parallel to the top of the rectangle.

✄Mark another horizontal line midway between the two lower lines.

✄Measure and vertically divide in half the pleat and whole scallop spaces.

✄Mark a dot at the center of the pleat on the shortest depth line. Mark a dot at the center of the whole scallop on the bottom line and another at the lower outside corner of the half-scallop.

✄Mark dots where the mid-depth line intersects the side edges of the pleat and the right side edge of the whole scallop.

✄Connect the dots in gentle curves. This line is the lower edge of the valance.

✄Divide the volume of one pleat by 4. In the half-scallop, measure and mark a line parallel to and this distance from the left of the pleat; this is the quarter-pleat return allowance for the end of the valance. To the left of this line, measure and mark the width of the board end return. (If the half-scallop is not sufficient for the pleat return and board return, extend it, and reverse the curve or not as seems appropriate). ▽

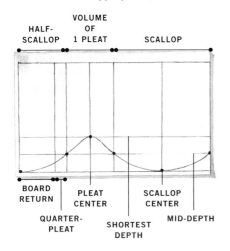

4 Add seam allowance to the left and bottom edges of the pattern; add the mounting allowance to the top edge. Cut out the pattern. Cut away the mounting allowance on top of the pleat space so you'll be able to reverse the pattern and easily mark the pleats later. ▷

5 If necessary, sew together the whole and partial widths for the valance (A) and the lining (A). Press the seams open.

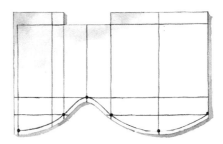

This design is an elegant choice for a traditional room. Without the panels the valance would work just as well over a row of kitchen windows.

pleated scalloped valance

A scalloped hemline gives this relatively easy box-pleated valance the look of a complicated trumpet valance.

6 Place the valance right side up on your worktable and mark the midpoint of the top edge. With the top edges aligned, place the pattern on the valance; align the midpoint of the whole scallop with the midpoint of the valance. Trace the bottom curve and the cutaway pleat top onto the fabric. Lift the pattern, move it to the left, align the right edge of the scallop with the left edge of the traced pleat, and repeat. ▽

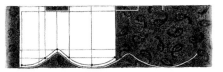

7 Repeat as necessary to the left edge of the valance, then turn the pattern over and repeat from the middle to the right edge. Cut out the valance, then use it as a pattern to cut out the lining.

TIPS FROM THE PROS
✂ Pin the valance to the lining and cut out both layers at once.

8 From the bias strips (B), make the welting (refer to Basics, page 115). With the right sides together and cut edges aligned, sew the welting to the side and lower edges of the valance.

9 With the right sides together and cut edges aligned, pin the lining to the valance. Sew together the lower and side edges. Trim the corners and clip the curves. △

10 Turn the valance right side out; press. Mark the top allowance line and baste the layers together on it.

11 Place the fabric right side up and fold it perpendicularly to the top allowance, to align each pair of pleat marks; pin each pleat through all thicknesses. Sew each pleat, stitching from the top allowance line toward the scallop for about 2". ▽

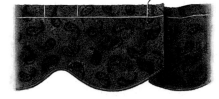

TIPS FROM THE PROS
✂ Test the fit of the pleated valance before you stitch the pleats. Adjust the pleat size a little if necessary.
✂ If you angle the pleat stitching line so it slants away from the pleat toward the lower edge, the pleats will hang in rounder trumpet shapes. If you do this, don't extend the stitching into the mounting allowance above each pleat.

12 Place the valance wrong side up on your ironing board. Center each seam over the pleat and press gently. Baste across the top of each pleat along the allowance line through all layers. ▽

TIPS FROM THE PROS
✂ If you slanted your pleat seams, the top allowance line may not align across the pressed pleats on the right side of the valance. Use the line on the scallop sections as your top alignment guide.

13 If desired, sew hook-and-loop tape to the wrong side of the top allowance. Otherwise, staple the valance to the mounting board (refer to page 109). Align the marked top allowance guide with the top edge of the board, and work from the center out to each side.

14 Install the mounting board.

TIPS FROM THE PROS

✂ The proportions of a swag like this are best judged from a sample. Follow the directions and make a mock-up from your fabric or muslin—cut it overly large and pushpin it to the top of the trim.

✂ The term *width* can be very confusing on a project like this. In the following directions, *width* refers to the dimension from tail tip to tail tip across the top of the window; *depth* refers to the dimension from the top of the window to the bottom of the swag. Cut your swag with the width on the lengthwise grain, the depth on the crosswise grain.

✂ The swag uses more fabric than you might expect—the sample measures 144" x 30". Avoid heavy fabrics; they'll be difficult to support and won't bunch attractively.

1 Make a schematic diagram for the swag as follows:

✂ To find the overall swag width, measure the top window trim from side to side. Then measure from the outside top corner of the window trim to the level desired for the lowest point of the swag tail and add 10"–15" for the pouf; double this sum. Add the result to the window width measurement. Enter the total in the panel length column of the length worksheet.

✂ Determine the depth for the swag, including some ease for draping, and enter this measurement in the panel width column of the width worksheet.

The secret to this soft swag? Don't worry your draping to perfection—the casual design is inherently charming.

ABOUT THE SAMPLE

This informal swag is just one length of fabric attached directly to the top of the window trim. At each corner the cloth is wrapped with elastic to form casual poufs on each side of a central drape. The fabric is lightweight linen, the bias-cut bows are silk shantung. Alternatively, this swag can be attached to the top of a mounting board that is installed with the broad face against the wall. Turn to page 65 for some variations on this design.

MATERIALS

Fabrics for swag and bow
Thread to match
Narrow hook-and-loop tape or dots (fusible if available) or thumbtacks
Narrow elastic, two 15" lengths

PLANNING

Refer to Part Three, Basics, for information on measuring, calculating yardage, mounting boards, and basic sewing techniques. Refer to step 1 to plan the dimensions of your swag.

MEASURE, MARK, AND CUT

Read the tips preceding steps 1 and 2. Add an allowance for a narrow hem to all four edges of the panel.

Ⓐ SWAG ✂ cut 1
Ⓑ BOW ✂ cut 4"-wide bias strips, sufficient to make two 60" lengths

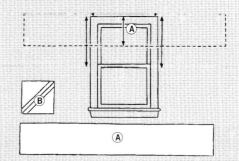

simple tied swag

Combine fabrics with as subtle or strong a contrast as you like; consider texture along with color. Here, pinking shears gave a quick and perky finish to crisp silk bows.

TIPS FROM THE PROS

✂This project is so simple you don't really have to fill in the worksheets unless you're planning to make multiple swags. Just add twice the hem allowance to each dimension planned in step 1, and cut out a rectangle of the resulting dimensions.

✂If you're making a mock-up, experiment with the swag proportions (or sketch them on a scale elevation). A wide window will look great with a shallow swag with short tails; a tall window like the one in the photo looks better with a deep swag and long tails.

2 Cut out the swag if you haven't already done so. Make a narrow hem on each edge.

TIPS FROM THE PROS

✂Corners on narrow hems can be difficult. Here are some tricks: Hem the ends of the swag first, and then hem the sides. Alternatively, round the corners slightly and make a continuous hem. Or sew tiny miters at the hem corners following the Designer Detail on page 44.

3 On one long edge of the swag, center and mark the dimension measured across the top of the window in step 1. Fuse or sew one half of the hook-and-loop tape to the hem between the marks.

✂If using hook-and-loop dots, space them 6"–8" apart.

TIPS FROM THE PROS

✂Alternatively, affix the swag with thumbtacks instead of hook-and-loop tape: In step 4, lift the fabric and insert the tacks through the wrong side of the top hem into the top of the window trim.

4 Fuse, glue, or staple the corresponding half of the hook-and-loop tape to the top face of the window trim. Position the swag over the window and press the two halves of the tape together.

✂If using dots, affix the corresponding pieces to the trim at the appropriate intervals. ▽

5 Place one hand on the lower edge of the swag where it begins to cascade, fold the edge under about 2", and then gently gather up the fabric, lifting it to the outside corner of the window trim above it. Scrunch the gathered fabric into a pouf and tie it tightly with one of the elastics. Don't worry about the pouf shape. ▽

6 Make a pouf at the other side of the swag. Pulling the fabric gently through the tied elastic, adjust the drape between the poufs. Then adjust the folds of the tails.

7 Tuck and twist the fabric in each pouf to create a nice shape. Pull the top edge of the fabric taut across the window trim to keep the poufs high. Cut off the excess elastic.

TIPS FROM THE PROS

✂If you find the poufs creep down after you've adjusted them, insert a pushpin into the trim through the elastic at the top of each pouf.

✂If you're using a very lightweight fabric and the poufs seem flimsy, tuck a little tulle or crushed tissue paper into each.

8 If you must piece the bias strips for the bows (B), place the seam at the midpoint of each. Cut the ends of the strips on the straight grain. Hem or otherwise finish all edges of each strip. Tie a bow around each pouf.

TIPS FROM THE PROS

✂If using a sheer fabric, make turned bias-cut tubes for the bows. (Refer to page 33 for a tube-turning tip.)

✂If you use pinking sheers to cut the strips you can leave them unhemmed.

✂You can use fabric cut on the straight grain instead of the bias for the bows, but it might not tie as gracefully.

other tied swags

With a little imagination you can drape and tie a swag in myriad ways. While there are several types of ready-made swag holders (just follow the manufacturer's directions), you don't need them to create effects like these. Follow the swag directions on pages 63–64 and make the adjustments indicated below. And don't hesitate to place an airy swag over matching panels or a summery roll-up shade.

ROSETTE TRIM

At the window corners, instead of tying poufs just slip the elastic under the fabric, wrap it around the full width, and tie. Arrange the central drape. Make coordinating rosettes (the directions are on pages 58–59) and pin or sew them over the elastic. ▷

LOOP TIE

For a truly simple swag, use a tassel tieback or other decorative trim to tie up the drape. Omit the pouf allowance from the overall width calculation. Fasten the tieback discreetly to the top of the window trim (use an upholstery tack) and tie around the full width of the fabric. ▷

DOUBLE DRAPE

Use two lengths of very lightweight fabric. After hemming each length, attach one to the top of the window. Then tie a pouf in the middle of the second length and place it, centered, over the first; hold it in place temporarily with pushpins. Working with both layers as one, form the poufs at the corners of the window. Remove the temporary pushpins and, if necessary, support each pouf with a hidden pushpin. (Alternatively, add the top layer over the loop-tied swag, lower left.) ▷

TIPS FROM THE PROS

✄ The top layer need not be as large as the bottom layer.
✄ Use lace or cotton net for one or both layers, or use contrasting-color sheers.

MULTIPLE ARC

This variation is particularly suitable for wide or multiple windows. For each arc you wish to add, make an additional, but shorter, bow strip. Before attaching the swag to the window, mark the arc intervals on the top edge of the fabric. Fold each short bow strip in half over the fabric edge at one of the marks. Attach the swag to the window, tie the bows, and form the poufs at the corners. Adjust all the drapes, retying the bows if necessary, and tie bows around the poufs. ▽

TIPS FROM THE PROS

✄ Before tying the shorter strips, lift each top tail and insert a thumbtack through the swag into the window trim.

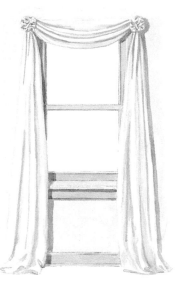

traditional
swag and tails

ABOUT THE SAMPLE

The face fabric for this fully lined swag and tails is woven with alternating matte and satin stripes. The upper edges are attached to the top of an inside-mounted board. The swag is mounted over the tails. On a wide window, use more than one swag.

MATERIALS

Fabrics for swag and tails and lining
Thread to match
Mounting board and hardware

PLANNING

Read Inside or Outside Mount?, page 94, then decide how your swag and tails will be mounted. Read the tips preceding the project directions, then decide the proportions of each component and make a schematic diagram for your design. Refer to Part Three, Basics, for information about measuring, calculating yardage, basic sewing techniques, and hardware.

MEASURE, MARK, AND CUT

Fill in the window treatment worksheets, page 104. Refer to the directions to make patterns. If making a pair of tails, be sure to reverse the pattern for one face piece and one lining.

Ⓐ SWAG ✄cut 1 for swag and 1 for lining
Ⓑ TAIL ✄cut 1 for each tail and 1 reversed for each lining

TIPS FROM THE PROS

✄The term *width* can be very confusing on a project like this. In the following directions, *width* refers to the dimension between the side edges of the swag, *depth* refers to the dimension between the upper and lower edges of the swag.

✄The longest depth of the swag in the photo is equal to $\frac{1}{4}$ the window-opening length. The width of each tail is equal to about $\frac{3}{5}$ the depth of the swag. The shorter depth of the tails is equal to 2 times the depth of the swag ($\frac{1}{2}$ the window-opening length), the longer depth to 3 times the swag depth ($\frac{3}{4}$ the window-opening length). Use proportions appropriate for your design.

✄Plan the pleats of the swag and tails to be the same depth.

✄The pattern on the swag and tail runs in the same direction. If using a directional fabric, be sure to cut the components so the pattern hangs as you wish.

NOTE: The project directions that follow are for making one lined swag and one lined tail. Repeat the appropriate directions for each additional element you want to make.

SWAG

1 To make a swag pattern, experiment with a piece of muslin that is 10" wider than the finished swag and 3 times as deep as the longest depth of the swag. Mark the mounting allowance at the top. Fold the muslin in half lengthwise, aligning the side edges, then mark and cut out the basic swag shape.

✄Measure away from the fold along the marked line a distance equal to $\frac{1}{2}$ the finished swag width; mark.

✄Draw a diagonal line connecting the lower corner opposite the fold, the upper mark, and the upper cut edge. ▽

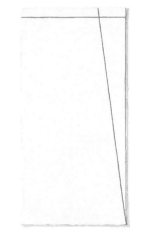

2 Cut out the muslin swag through both layers along the diagonal line.

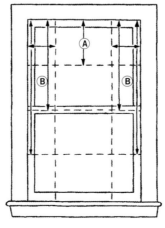

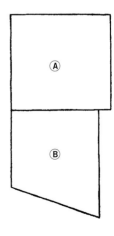

3 Unfold the muslin and mark the vertical center along the foldline. Press out the fold. Decide how many pleats you'd like. Increase this number by 1, and divide it into the length of the diagonal line. (For five pleats, divide the line by 6.) The result is the pleat interval. Measuring below the mounting allowance, mark the interval along each diagonal edge. ▽

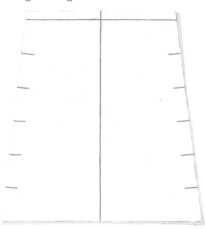

TIPS FROM THE PROS

✄If the division results in an awkward pleat interval, round the number down to the next workable fraction; place the excess at the bottom of the diagonal line.

4 Pin the mounting allowance of the muslin to the straight side edge of your ironing board (or the side edge of any surface into which you can insert pushpins and below which the fabric can hang free). So that you'll be able to see the finished width as you pleat the muslin, insert two pins into the top of the board, placing one directly above the intersection of the marked allowance line and each cut side edge of the muslin.

A pleated swag over pleated tails will impart a period feeling to virtually any decor. Here the single-panel sheer trimmed with gold tassel fringe is a graceful addition.

5 At one side edge, pinch a fold at the first mark below the allowance, then bring the fold up and toward the center until the fold is almost perpendicular to the upper edge of the muslin and the point is about 1" above the upper edge; pin to the board. (Unpin the ends of the mounting allowance as necessary to do this.) Pinch and fold the corresponding mark on the opposite side edge, coaxing the pleat into a rounded fold; pin.

6 Working downward, repeat at each mark to form staggered pleats, making each fold more relaxed than the previous one. The center line should fall straight through each fold. Along the sides, the concealed bottom folds of the pleats should not extend beyond the pins marking the finished swag width; any excess muslin on the lower edge will be cut off when you refine the curve. ▽

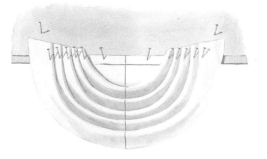

7 Step back and look at your swag. Adjust the pleats and repin them until you are pleased. The overall look is more important than perfect symmetry—you'll true up the shape before you cut it in the final fabric.

TIPS FROM THE PROS

✄If you're not pleased, consider making fewer, deeper pleats, or more, shallower pleats. Or, make the overall swag more or less deep.

✄The farther in toward the center the pleats are pinned, the more deeply they will drape.

8 Compare the left and right halves of the swag. Decide which half you prefer.

✄On the preferred half, check that the fold of the bottom pleat doesn't extend beyond the marker pin on the top of the board; repin if needed. Using a straightedge, mark lines to extend the cut edge of the allowance and the marked allowance line across the pleats on both halves of the swag.

✄On the lower marked line, directly below each marker pin on the top of the board, make a dot to mark the width of the finished swag.

✄On the mounting allowance, mark the alignment of the innermost pleats.

TIPS FROM THE PROS

✄If the vertical line marking the center of the swag has shifted but you like the swag shape, mark a new center line perpendicular to the top edge.

Note the symmetrical positioning of these stripes. Avoid fabrics with asymmetrical repeats; they'll be impossible to balance.

9 Pin the pleats to themselves, then remove the muslin from the board with the pleats intact. Trim the open edges of the pleats on the marked cut-edge line and remove the pins.

✄On the preferred half of the swag, make a cut straight down through the mounting allowance to the dot on the marked allowance line. Then, turn the swag wrong side up and trim away any excess fabric, using the lowest pleat fold (indicated by the dotted line in the illustration) as a guide. ▽

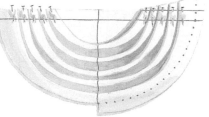

10 Fold the muslin in half along the center line, then cut the untrimmed half of the swag to match the trimmed half.

11 To double-check the shape, repin the swag to the board, aligning the zigzag cut edges to pleat both sides as before; align the innermost pleats as marked on the mounting allowance. Make any needed adjustments and re-mark the muslin as necessary, then remove it from the board. Unpin the muslin, flatten it, and measure the greatest width and depth; transfer the dimensions to the worksheets.

12 Cut the muslin in half along the center line. Use the preferred half to mark a half swag pattern on paper. Add seam allowance at the lower edge and cut out the pattern. ▽

TIPS FROM THE PROS

✂ You can use the muslin as a pattern, just be sure to add seam allowance along the lower edge before you cut the swag fabrics.

✂ Your fabric may drape somewhat differently from the muslin. If you cut the swag with extra seam allowance along the pleated edges, you'll be able to adjust the draping if you wish.

✂ If making multiple swags, make a test swag in your fabrics before cutting out all of the pieces.

13 Cut out the swag and lining. With the right sides together and cut edges aligned, pin the lining to the swag. Sew together the lower edges.

14 Turn the swag right side out. Align the cut edges; press. Pin the layers together. On the front of the swag, mark the mounting allowance with tailor's chalk, then baste the layers together. Mark a line along the vertical center.

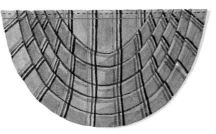

15 Working with the fabrics as a single layer, pin the pleats as before. Check that the center line hangs straight, adjust the pleats as needed, then baste the top through all layers; topstitch. Brush away the center line. △

TAIL

1 To find the cut size of your tail, first decide how wide you want it to be when pleated. On a piece of scrap paper, draw a vertical rectangle and write the width on the top edge. Parallel to one side, draw three lines to represent the outside folds of the pleats. Label the spaces X, Y, Y, and Y as shown. X is the top pleat; decide how wide it should be. Subtract X from the total width, and divide the remainder by 3 to find Y. ▽

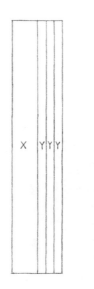

2 Make a full-size muslin or paper pattern for the tail. Refer to the diagrams below and on the next page and use an L-square to be sure your lines are true.

✂ The finished unpleated width of the tail is equal to 7X plus 4Y. Calculate this sum and draw a line this length to represent the top of the tail. (If you want more than three pleats, add 2X plus Y for each additional pleat.)

✂ Decide how long the tail should be at its longest point, then at each end of the top line draw a perpendicular line this length. Draw another line parallel to the top to make a rectangle. Draw the top allowance above the top line and add ½" seam allowance outside the remaining edges.

✂ Draw lines perpendicular to the top line, spacing them at the X and Y intervals shown on the diagram.

✂ Referring to the diagram, label the appropriate lines O/F (outside fold) and I/F (inside fold). ▽

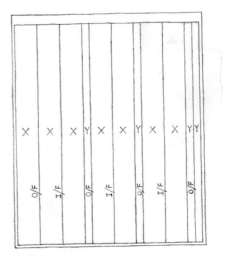

traditional swag and tails

✂Cut out the rectangle on the outer lines and fold it accordion-style on the marked foldlines so that the outside X space is on the top of the stack of pleats and the outside Y space is on the bottom—it should look like the first diagram you drew. (Note that the outside Y space will be the return of the tail; you can make it wider or omit it as desired.)

✂Decide how long the tail should be at its shallowest point. Measure this distance from the top-edge line and mark it on the free edge of the X space. Unfold the pattern and draw a diagonal line from the mark to the opposite lower corner of the outside Y space. Draw a $1/2$" seam allowance parallel to this last line, and cut along the outer line. Slash the pattern along the fold lines through the top allowance for reference later. ▽

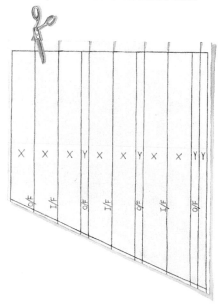

✂Fill in the overall width and depth on your worksheets.

TIPS FROM THE PROS

✂Tape the pleated pattern over your window to check the proportions. Lengthen or shorten the tail at the top edge, or cut a different angle at the bottom. For the best preview, place the muslin swag over the tail.

3 Cut out the tail and lining.

4 With the right sides together and cut edges aligned, pin the lining to the tail. Sew together the lower and side edges. Trim the seam allowance across the lower corners.

5 Turn the tail right side out. Align the cut edges; press. Pin the layers together at the top. On the front of the tail, mark the mounting allowance with tailor's chalk, then baste the layers together. Place the tail right side up on your worktable and, aligning the top edges, place the pattern on top of the tail. Mark the position of the folds through the slashed lines on the pattern.

6 With the tail right side up, pin the pleats as you did for the muslin. Baste across the top of the tail through all layers; topstitch. ▷

TIPS FROM THE PROS

✂Be sure to maintain the inside and outside fold orientation as planned, otherwise the lining will end up on the outside.

✂Press the folds before installation for a crisp look.

Choose a lining fabric with the same hand as the face fabric for pleated treatments such as this. To ensure that the diagonal edge turns neatly, avoid bulky fabrics.

HANGING

1 With the tail right side up, place the mounting allowance on the top face of the mounting board, aligning the marked line with the top edge of the board. The cascades should face front, the long side edge should be at the end of the board, and the side edges should be aligned. Staple in place. Repeat for the other tail.

2 With the swag right side up, place the mounting allowance on the top face of the mounting board over the tails. Staple in place.

3 Install the board.

TIPS FROM THE PROS

✂For an outside mount, you can attach the swag and tails to the top of the board with hook-and-loop tape so that they are easily removable for laundering.

swag and tail **arrangements**

When dressing a window with classic swags and tails you have a number of design options. This is especially true when the window opening is wide. The options can be as simple as mounting the tails on top of or under the swag. More elaborate schemes include overlapping swags, alternating swags and tails, or tails of varied lengths.

Here are some guidelines for planning the dimensions of multiple swag-and-tail arrangements; always make a sketch and begin with the total width of the treatment:

✂Usually you don't account for the tail width when figuring the swag width. Swags mounted over tails must extend to the edge of the board. However, swags mounted under tails can be inset from the board ends; in this case, total the extending tail width (at both ends of the board) and subtract from the total treatment width before calculating the swag width.

✂To find the swag width when the design consists of swags meeting edge to edge across the window, divide the number of swags into the treatment width. (Do this even when the swags meet under tails or other swags.)

✂To find the swag width when the design consists of one fully revealed swag and several overlapping swags, count the number of half swags, add 1, and divide the treatment width by the total.

✂If using swags on corner or bay windows, be sure to measure the treatment width at a distance in front of the window equal to the depth of the mounting board. (Refer to Basics, page 96.)

tailored scarf swag

Painted wood holdbacks suit the country-check fabric on this old door. You'll find lots of holdback options, so choose a style that is in character with your decor.

ABOUT THE SAMPLE

This reversible scarf swag was made from a sturdy cotton check with a solid lining. It is a trapezoid of fabric, folded into accordion pleats and placed over decorative holdbacks mounted above the window.

MATERIALS

Fabrics for swag and lining
Thread to match
Holdbacks and hardware

PLANNING

Refer to Part Three, Basics, for information on measuring, calculating yardage, basic sewing techniques, and hardware. Refer to step 1 to plan the dimensions of your swag.

MEASURE, MARK, AND CUT

Fill in the window treatment worksheets, page 104.

(A) **SWAG** ✂cut 1 for swag and 1 for lining

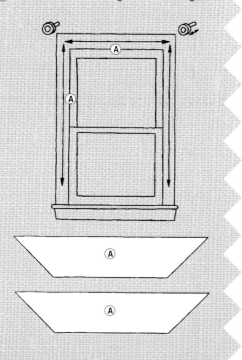

TIPS FROM THE PROS

✂Once you've figured out the proportions for a pleated scarf swag, the sewing is a snap. If you have a good sense of proportion, you can calculate the size from a schematic drawing—follow step 1 and draw the shape on paper, noting the dimensions. When ready, draft the swag full-size directly on your fabric.

✂The term *width* can be very confusing on a project like this. In the following directions, *width* refers to the dimension from tail tip to tail tip across the top of the window, *depth* refers to the dimension from front to back. If you are using a fabric with a vertical pattern, cut the swag width on the lengthwise grain.

NOTE: The directions that follow are for making one lined swag. Repeat the directions for each additional swag you want to make.

1 Make a muslin mock-up for your swag. First install the holdbacks and measure the distance between them to find the swag center width.

✂To find the overall width, decide on the length of the tail from the holdback to the lowest point; double this number and add it to the swag center width.

✂Cut a piece of muslin the length of the overall swag width and fold it in half crosswise. Mark the top selvage to represent the longest edge of the swag.

✂To find the swag depth, measure the length of the holdback posts to find the depth of one pleat. Decide on the number of pleats (usually 3 or 4) and multiply this number by 2 times the pleat depth. Measuring along the foldline, mark this distance from the top selvage.

✂Decide the length of the tail from the holdback to the highest point. Add this number to half the swag center width. Draw a line the length of the resulting number perpendicular to the fold at the swag-depth mark on the muslin. This line will be the swag edge between the highest points of the tails.

✂Draw a diagonal line between the end of this line and the corner of the muslin on the top selvage. ▽

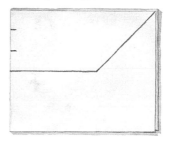

✂Cut out the muslin through both layers. Unfold it and, folding back and forth at the interval chosen for your pleat depth, make accordion pleats parallel to the long edge. ▽

✄Place the pleated muslin, centered and with the long edge toward the wall, over the holdbacks. If the tails are too long, shorten them by unfolding the muslin and cutting away the desired amount along the angled edges. If the tails are too short, cut the muslin on the center (depth) foldline and piece in a strip wide enough to add the desired length.

2 When you are satisfied with the proportions of the swag, measure the longest edge, add 2" for seam allowance (because of the angle, 1" won't be enough) and transfer the total to the cut width column of the width worksheet. Measure the depth of the muslin, add 1" for seam allowance, and transfer the total to the cut length column of the length worksheet. Complete the worksheets and purchase your fabric.

3 Using your muslin as a pattern and adding seam allowance all around, cut out the swag and lining.

4 With the right sides together and cut edges aligned, pin and sew the lining to the swag; leave an opening for turning on one of the straight-grain edges. Trim the seam allowance at the corners and turn the swag right side out; press. Press the seam allowance to the inside at the opening, and slipstitch the opening closed. ▽

5 Pleat the swag as you did the muslin mock-up, folding at the interval chosen for your pleat depth and making accordion pleats parallel to the long edge.

TIPS FROM THE PROS
✄Whichever fabric side faces up before you begin folding will peek from inside the cascading tails when the swag is in the holdbacks. △

6 Place the pleated swag over the holdbacks so the tails hang equally on both sides. If desired, adjust the swag, pulling gently on the lower folds to increase the depth and on the upper folds to keep the top nearly straight.

TIPS FROM THE PROS
✄Press the folds before installation for a crisp look.
✄If the swag is installed with the longest pleat on top, the cascades will face each other on the inside of the reveal, as shown in the photo. If the swag is installed with the shortest pleat on top, the cascades will be on the outside of the reveal.

This informal design looks good on windows of almost any proportion—center a third holdback on the top of an extra-wide window.

scarf swag

ABOUT THE SAMPLE

The swag is an isosceles triangle (two sides are equal in length). The chintz ruffle is folded in half lengthwise, gathered, and inserted between the face fabric and lining. The cotton print sample is cut on the bias, which may be inappropriate for some fabrics. To make the matching rod-pocket panels and sleeve, refer to Basic Rod-Pocket Panels, Rod Pockets and Headings, and Rod Sleeves, pages 30–33, and include a heading.

MATERIALS

Fabrics for swag, lining, and ruffle
Thread to match
Curtain rod or pole with finials
Mounting hardware

PLANNING

Refer to Part Three, Basics, for information on measuring, calculating yardage, ruffles and other basic sewing techniques, and hardware. Refer to steps 1 and 2 to plan and measure for your swag.

MEASURE, MARK, AND CUT

Fill in the window treatment worksheets, page 104. Refer to your schematic to mark and cut the swag, adding seam allowance all around. Cut the ruffle to twice the desired finished depth plus seam allowance, cutting on the bias or straight grain as desired.

Ⓐ **SWAG** ✂cut 1 for swag and 1 for lining
Ⓑ **RUFFLE** ✂cut enough strips to gather and then rim the swag

1 Refer to the diagram below to make a schematic plan; it need not bc in scalc. The hypotenuse of the triangle is the top edge of the swag; the corners drape over the curtain pole to form tails.
✂To calculate the dimension of the top edge of the swag, measure the distance between the pole brackets and add to it twice the desired length of the tails.
✂Decide how deep you want the swag to be at its center, including some drape. ▽

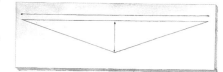

2 Decide on which grain to cut the swag. Then complete the worksheets as follows, and purchase your fabric.
✂If the hypotenuse will be on the lengthwise grain, write its dimension in the length column of the length worksheet and write the dimension of the swag depth in the panel width column of the width worksheet.
✂If swag depth will be on the lengthwise grain, write its dimension in the length column of the length worksheet and write the dimension of the hypotenuse in the panel width column of the width worksheet. You might have to piece the swag width.
✂If the hypotenuse will be on the bias, you must do some math to find the

The little chintz ruffle gives a pretty finish to this swag, but beware—the ruffle is many yards long before it's gathered.

required fabric yardage: Calculate the square of the hypotenuse, divide by 2, take the square root of this number and use the result as both the length and panel width on the worksheets (shown by the dotted line on the schematic below). If the hypotenuse is longer than the bias of the usable width of your fabric, piece it on the bias; try to make the center section width equal to the distance between the pole brackets.

TIPS FROM THE PROS

✂To be safe, add a total of 2" to each dimension for seam allowance (because of the angles, 1" won't be enough).

3 Refer to your schematic to draft the triangle directly onto your fabrics. Add seam allowance all around and cut out. If necessary, sew together the whole and partial widths for the swag (A) and lining (A).

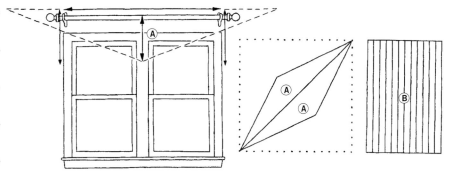

✄For a straight-grain swag, fold the fabric along the swag depth; draft a half swag and cut out through both layers. Then use the cut-out swag as a pattern to cut out the lining.

4 Gently drape one of the triangles over your curtain pole. If the tails are too bulky, reshape the lower edges as shown. ▽

A large triangle of fabric makes a striking scarf swag. Also consider finishing the edges with welting, bias binding, or braid.

5 Cut out and sew together the ruffle pieces to make a ring. Press all seams open. Press the ruffle in half lengthwise, right side out, aligning the cut edges; pin and baste the cut edge closed.

TIPS FROM THE PROS

✄Whether the ruffle is cut on the bias or straight grain, to reduce bulk after folding always cut and sew the ends of the strips on a 45-degree angle.

6 Fold the ruffle in quarters and mark each fold near the cut edge. Gather the cut edge in sections as marked (refer to Basics, pages 114–15).

7 Measure, divide, and mark the perimeter of the swag into four equal sections; the sections need not align with any specific points on the perimeter.

TIPS FROM THE PROS

✄The ruffle will be easier to handle if you continue to subdivide the edges. Divide the swag into the same number of sections. Pin marks will be easier to find than chalk marks, but are likely to fall out.

8 Arrange the ruffle on the right side of the swag, aligning the cut edges and matching the marks; pin. ▽

TIPS FROM THE PROS

✄To prevent the edges of the swag from stretching, staystitch them before pinning on the ruffle.

9 Pull up the basting threads so the ruffle fits the swag edge. Adjust the fullness evenly but place some extra at each point (corner) so the ruffle will fan out when pressed away from the point; pin. Sew the ruffle to the swag.

10 With the right sides together and cut edges aligned, pin and sew the lining to the swag; leave an opening in the hypotenuse edge. Trim the seam allowance at the points and turn the swag right side out. Press the seam allowance to the inside at the opening and slipstitch the opening closed.

11 Center the swag on the pole and drape the ends behind the finials.

roman shade

ABOUT THE SAMPLE

The folds on this Roman shade are suspended from ribbons sewn to the back of the pleats; rings sewn to the ribbons guide the cords that raise the shade. As the shade is raised, the pleats refold and align with the lower edge of the skirt. Dowels can be inserted at the top of each pleat, a lath can be added to the lower edge of the skirt (refer to the tips following step 2). To make a flat Roman shade, turn to the Design Variation on page 79.

MATERIALS

Fabric

Ribbon or twill tape

Thread to match

Wood lath and dowels (optional)

Small curtain rings

Shade cord

Mounting board and hardware

Screw eyes

Cord pull and cleat

PLANNING

Read Inside or Outside Mount?, page 94, and Mounting Boards, page 108, then decide how your shade will be mounted. Read all of the project directions before beginning. Read steps 1 and 2 to plan your shade. Refer to Part Three, Basics, for information on measuring, calculating yardage, basic sewing techniques, and hardware.

MEASURE, MARK, AND CUT

Fill in the window treatment worksheets, page 104.

Ⓐ **SHADE** ✂ **cut 1 for each shade**

NOTE: The directions that follow are for making one shade. Repeat the directions for each additional shade you want to make.

TIPS FROM THE PROS

✂No matter how precisely you figure this shade, the thickness of your fabric may alter the overall length. Cut the shade a little longer than needed, complete steps 1–8, then pin one ribbon all the way up the back of the shade as described in steps 9 and 10, and check to see that the length from the mounting allowance line to the lower edge equals the wall space length noted on your sketch. Adjust the spacing on all the ribbons or at the top of the shade as necessary.

1 To begin, make a sketch of the window and note the length and width of the wall space the shade (A) will cover. Decide how many pleats your shade will have, then, referring to the diagram above right and working as follows, make a schematic diagram of the flat (unpleated) shade. The schematic need not be to scale, but it will be easier to follow if you sketch approximate proportions.

✂For the schematic, draw a horizontal space for each pleat; label each Y. At the bottom, draw another space about half as deep as the others for the skirt;

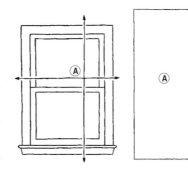

---

label it X. At the top, draw another space for the thickness of the board. ✂Calculate the shade width appropriately for an inside or outside mount, and fill in the width worksheet. ▽

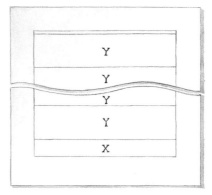

TIPS FROM THE PROS

✂The calculations required to determine the pleat proportions make this shade seem more complicated than it is. Here's a front view of the lowered shade showing the relationships; the dotted lines represent the top edge of each interval: ▽

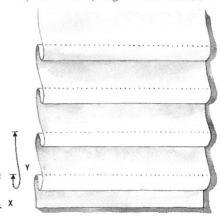

X = SKIRT DEPTH
Y = PLEAT INTERVAL
2X = Y
THE SOFT FOLD USES HALF THE PLEAT INTERVAL

2 Use a calculator to work out the cut length dimensions. Don't worry if the skirt depth works out to an awkward decimal place, you'll round it down to a

workable fraction before you actually
mark the skirt and pleats on the fabric;
you'll then place any excess at the top
of the shade. Note your dimensions off
to the side of the schematic so you can
refer to them later. The examples given
in parentheses are for a 51" wall space
length and 4 pleats.

✂ First subtract the thickness of your
mounting board from the wall space length
to find the available length; don't forget
that outside-mounted boards are installed
with the wide face against the wall.
(51" – 1" thickness = 50" available length.)

✂ Divide the available length by the
number of pleats plus 1. The result is
the skirt depth/raised pleat depth.
(50" ÷ 5 = 10" skirt depth.)

✂ Multiply the number of pleats by
the skirt depth. Add the result to the
available length.
(4 pleats x 10" skirt depth = 40";
40" + 50" = 90".)

✂ Add the thickness of the board to this
figure and place the total in the panel
length column of the length worksheet.
(90" + 1" = 91" panel length.)

✂ Add the mounting allowance and
bottom hem allowance to the schematic
and to the worksheet.

TIPS FROM THE PROS

✂ For a sheer fabric, make the bottom
hem equal to the skirt depth. Don't
miter the corners.

✂ If you wish to use a bottom lath,
include an appropriate rod-pocket
allowance (refer to Basics, page 99).

✂ Plan to insert a thin dowel or plastic rod
at the top of each pleat if you'd like the
top folds to be rigid (these are the folds
on the wrong side of the shade to which
the rings will be attached). To allow for the

Soft, loose folds march regularly down the
front of these shades even when they are
fully lowered. To see this design in another
fabrication, turn to page 55.

dowels, calculate a rod-pocket allowance,
multiply by the number of pleats, and
add the total to the panel length before
adding the top and bottom allowances.

3 Cut out the shade. Hem the side and
bottom edges, making a pocket for a
lath if desired.

4 For you to easily mark the pleat
intervals on your shade, the skirt depth
should end in a whole or fractional
measurement you can see on your ruler.

✂ Adjust the decimal interval noted on
your schematic down to the next $1/8$" or
$1/4$" increment and use this figure as
your actual skirt depth; write it on the
skirt portion of the schematic.

✂ Multiply the number by 2 and use the
result as the actual pleat interval; write
this figure on each pleat section of the
schematic.

✂ If you want to include a dowel at the
top of each pleat, add half the rod-pocket
allowance to the skirt depth and also to

the pleat interval before adjusting the
measurement down.

5 Place the shade wrong side up,
then refer to your schematic and the
first illustration on the next page to
mark the skirt depth above the bottom
edge. Measure and mark at the side
edges and twice in between; connect
the marks. In the same way, measure
and mark the appropriate number of
pleat intervals above the skirt. Then
measure down from the cut edge to
mark the top mounting allowance. If your
pleat interval was adjusted, the extra
space between the top pleat interval
and the mounting allowance will be
greater than the thickness of the board.

✂ Check that the lines are parallel to the
upper and lower edges of the shade.

soft-fold roman shade

6 While the shade is still wrong side up, determine the placement of the ribbons that will suspend the soft pleats when the shade is lowered. The outer ribbons should be 4"–6" in from the side edges so the pleats will appear to float along the sides of the shade. Additional ribbons should go between these at a 9"–14" interval; space them evenly. ✄Measure and mark the spacing along three or four of the marked horizontal lines; connect the marks vertically, extending them to the top and bottom edges. ▽

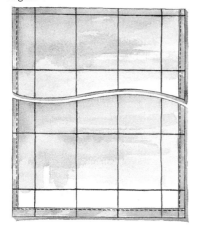

7 Fold the shade, right side in, along the horizontal line marked at the top of the skirt. Edgestitch the fold, or stitch the appropriate distance from the fold to make the dowel pocket. Repeat on each pleat interval line except the top one. ▽

8 For each marked vertical line, cut a ribbon the length of the wall space plus mounting allowance. Fold under 1" at one end of each ribbon and topstitch $1/2$" from the fold. On the right side of the ribbon, measure up from the topstitching and mark at intervals equal to the skirt depth/raised pleat depth; make a mark for each pleat, including the topstitching as one mark.

9 Place the shade on your worktable right side up with the skirt facing away from you. Fold back the skirt along the edgestitched fold. Position a ribbon, right side up and topstitched end toward the skirt hem, over one of the marked vertical lines; align the topstitching on the ribbon with the fold of the skirt, and pin. In the same way, pin the remaining ribbons to the skirt fold on the remaining vertical lines. Stitch each ribbon to the shade through all layers along the edgestitching (or rod-pocket stitching) line.

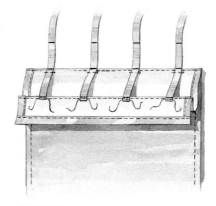

10 With the right side up as before, fold back the shade on the next stitched horizontal fold. Align the next mark on each ribbon with this fold, raising the fold at the top of the skirt and forming a pleat across the shade as you do so. Pin and stitch each ribbon as before. △

The soft folds make this design a little less tailored than a flat Roman shade.

11 In the same way continue to refold the shade and align and stitch the ribbon to each subsequent fold. ✄For the top pleat, align the mark on the ribbon with the top marked pleat interval line, then smooth the ribbon to the top of the shade and stitch together along the mounting allowance line.

12 Sew a ring to each ribbon at each fold on the back of the shade; align the top arc of each ring with the stitching across the ribbon (refer to Basics, page 117). ▽

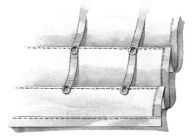

13 Referring to Basics, page 109, attach the shade to the mounting board, install the screw eyes, and cut and thread the shade cords.

14 Install the mounting board. Finish rigging the shade, passing the cords through the screw eyes, adjusting the tension, and finishing the ends with a cord pull. Install the cleat on the appropriate side of the window. ✄If using a lath and/or dowels, slip each into the appropriate pocket.

flat **roman shades**

These pleat-up fabric shades are wonderfully adaptable. Used alone, their effect is usually sporty or tailored; under another treatment, they add sophistication and a true custom finish. Following is the basic method plus some ideas for altering their appearance. Some of these variations can also be used on roller shades.

FLAT ROMAN SHADE

To make a traditional Roman shade, first make a flat shade sized to cover your window, plus top mounting allowance. Divide the window length by the desired skirt depth (raised pleat depth); the result must be a whole odd number. If it is not, adjust the skirt depth and divide again. On the wrong side of the shade, mark three or more vertical guidelines for the rings parallel to the side edges. On each, measure and mark the skirt depth above the bottom edge; above this, mark at an interval equal to 2 times the skirt depth. Sew a ring at each mark. Refer to Basics, pages 108–110, to rig the shade.

TIPS FROM THE PROS

✄If your division results in an odd number with a small decimal surplus (5.3 for instance), go ahead and use that skirt depth; the excess will not be apparent at the top of the shade.

SHAPED HEMLINE

Cut a curve, scallop, point, or zigzag into the lower edge and finish it with a facing or binding. Place the lowest rigging rings at least one full pleat interval above the lower edge so the skirt will extend below the pleats. Make a casing or lath pocket just below the rings instead of at the bottom edge. ▷

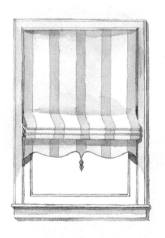

TRIMMED HEMLINE

Add ball or tassel fringe or a short, flirty ruffle to the lower edge. For best results, insert the trim between the face fabric and a facing so the wrong side of the shade looks neat. For a ruffle, fold the fabric double so it doesn't need to be hemmed.

TABBED HEMLINE

Instead of stiffening the lower edge with a concealed lath, add tabs and hang a decorative rod through them. For an inside mount, be sure the rod finials will fit between the edge of the shade and the window reveal. ▷

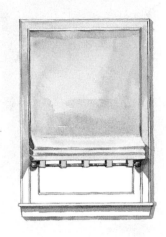

CONTRAST TRIM

Add one or more bands of trim or ribbon parallel to and several inches inside the edges. If you want the trim to parallel all three edges, miter the lower corners for a neat finish. Be sure the trim is as flat as possible so the shade pleats up neatly.

FAN SHADE

This design is most graceful when made in sheer or lightweight fabric. Make a flat Roman shade but use only a center column of rigging rings. Make the interval between the rings smaller than usual to create a dainty fan. ▷

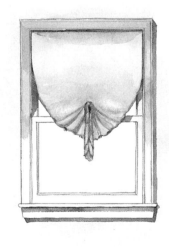

poufed
cloud shade

ABOUT THE SAMPLE

This cloud shade is really a cross between a rod-pocket curtain and a pull-up shade. It is inside-mounted on a continental (flat) rod with returns; there is a deep heading above the rod pocket. A dowel in a pocket at the lower edge controls the fullness. The screw eyes that carry the rigging are inserted directly into the top reveal of the window; for an outside mount, you'll need a mounting board as well as a rod.

MATERIALS

Fabric
Thread to match
Continental rod and mounting hardware
Dowel
Small curtain rings
Screw eyes
Shade cord
Cord pull and cleat

PLANNING

Read Inside or Outside Mount?, page 94, and Mounting Boards, page 108, then decide how your shade will be mounted. Read Measuring for a Rod Pocket, page 99. Read step 1 and make a schematic diagram for your shade. Refer to Part Three, Basics, for information on measuring, calculating yardage, basic sewing techniques, and hardware.

MEASURE, MARK, AND CUT

Fill in the window treatment worksheets, page 104. If you are dressing multiple windows, be sure to fill out worksheets for each different size window.

Ⓐ **SHADE** ✂ cut 1

NOTE: The directions that follow are for making one shade. Repeat the directions for each additional shade you want to make.

TIPS FROM THE PROS

✂ You can make a stationary cloud valance following these same directions. Instead of rigging the shade through screw eyes, just thread the cords through the rings, pull the cords up so the shade is the desired length, and tie each cord to itself. You would probably want to cut a shorter length for a valance than for an adjustable shade.

1 On this cloud shade the lower edge is folded up to the wrong side and permanently tied to the rigging rings, creating a poufed hemline. Determine the length, width, fullness, and rod-pocket and heading allowances for your shade (A) as you would for any rod-pocket curtain, but add 7"–10" extra length for the pouf and the bottom dowel pocket (refer to Rod Pockets and Headings, page 32). Note each measurement on your schematic.

✂ If you omit the dowel, the lower edge of a cloud shade will fall in looser scallops. Refer to the Design Variations on page 83.

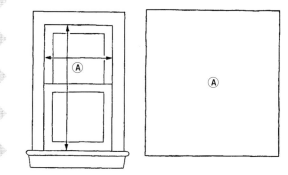

TIPS FROM THE PROS

✂ The length of the pouf allowance will be half the vertical interval between the rigging rings (refer to step 5); add the appropriate dowel-pocket allowance to this measurement.

✂ When the shade is lowered, the visual length is measured from the upper edge of the heading to the bottom of the pouf. Increase the length if you'd like to have more draping when the shade is lowered. Err on the long side—you want to be sure the window is covered.

2 Cut out the whole and partial widths as needed. Sew them together. Hem the side edges of the shade.

TIPS FROM THE PROS

✂ Use French or flat-felled seams so the wrong side of the shade will be attractive.

3 Mark and stitch the rod pockets.

✂ For the upper pocket, add together the rod-pocket depth, heading depth, and the $3/4$" hem allowance and stitching margin. On the front of the shade, mark a line this distance below and parallel to the top edge.

✂ For the lower pocket, add together the dowel-pocket depth plus the $3/4$" hem allowance and stitching margin. Mark a line this distance above and parallel to the lower edge.

✂ Fold $1/2$" to the wrong side along the upper edge of the shade and press. Fold the fabric to the wrong side again along the marked line and press. Topstitch through all layers along the first fold. Repeat for the lower edge.

4 Measure, mark, and topstitch the upper heading. ▽

5 Determine the placement of the rings on the wrong side of the shade and attach them.

✂Just above the dowel pocket, measure in 1"–3" (or at least half the diameter of the rings) from the side edges; mark with pins or chalk.

✂Measure the width of the shade between the marks, then divide that figure by the desired number of scallops to arrive at the horizontal interval between the rings; mark the intervals. Measure and mark the same intervals across the shade just below the upper hem and twice more in between the hems.

✂Use tailor's chalk to draw vertical lines between the hems to connect the marks.

✂Measure up along each vertical line and mark appropriate intervals for the rings (usually 9"–11"). Make the top mark at least a full interval below the top hem.

✂Check that the vertical rows are parallel to the side edges and the horizontal rows are aligned. Sew the rings to the shade. ▷

Cloud shades have both horizontal and vertical fullness, so by nature they're somewhat exuberant. A large-scale plaid is used with great effect on this set.

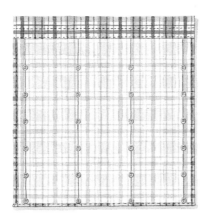

TIPS FROM THE PROS

✂The stitches will show on the front. Use doubled heavy-duty thread that matches and make neat stitches. A buttonhole stitch is strongest (refer to Basics, page 118). If you've lined your shade, be sure to sew through all layers.

✂If you prefer to use ring tape, sew the rings, not the tape, to the shade to avoid creating vertical rows of stitching on the front.

✂Iron-on ring tape is an alternative; test it first on a scrap of your fabric.

poufed cloud shade

6 Slip the dowel into the lower pocket, gathering the fabric evenly. To prevent the fabric from wandering, on the wrong side of the shade staple the gathers onto the dowel at the ends and at 12"–18" intervals (or use upholstery tacks). ▽

7 Position the screw eyes: On the inside top reveal of the window or the bottom of the mounting board, as appropriate to your situation, measure and mark intervals to correspond to the ring column intervals on the shade. Insert the screw eyes.

When you raise or lower a cloud shade, take a moment to adjust the poufs—they may not fall into perfect shapes by themselves. Soft fabric will hang in limp poufs.

8 Refer to Rigging the Board, page 109, and then cut a length of shade cord for each column of rings. Turn the shade wrong side up and thread the cord from bottom to top through each column. Fold the dowel edge up, bringing the two lower rows of rings together, and tie each cord to itself. ▷

9 Slip the curtain rod through the pocket, gathering the fabric evenly on the front and returns. Install the rod.

10 Finish rigging the shade, passing the cords through the screw eyes, adjusting the tension, and finishing the ends with a cord pull. Install the cleat on the appropriate side of the window.

other **cloud shades**

On a classic cloud shade, the shade is not gathered at the lower edge. When the shade is raised, gravity causes the fullness to drape in scallops between the vertical cords. To make any of these designs follow the directions for the Poufed Cloud Shade on pages 80–82, omitting the dowel pocket at the lower edge, making a regular hem, and incorporating any other instructions given with each illustration. Omit the heading if you wish.

TIPS FROM THE PROS

✄ The wider the space between the columns of rings, the more swagged the drape of the scallop will be. When the space is narrower, the scallops will hang in smoother poufs.

✄ The greater the overall fullness, the more voluminous the swagging will be. Assess the hand of your fabric and the effect desired—more is not necessarily prettier.

✄ These shades are often cut extra-long so that three or four rings can be tied together to create generously draped scallops even when the shade is down.

✄ To create a deeper scallop in the center and shallower scallops at the sides, tie together more rings in the column on each side edge of the shade, fewer in the column on each side of the center scallop.

TAILED SHADE

When the rigging is omitted from the side edges of a cloud shade, there is nothing to pull the outer sections up into scallops—instead the pleats fan open from the interior rigging toward the sides. On narrow windows, tailed shades usually have only one central scallop and a tail width that is no greater than half the scallop width. On wider windows, they can have more scallops. ▷

The wider the tails, the longer they'll be—if they're wider than half the scallop width, the lower corners of the shade will hang below the lowest arc of the scallop.

SKIRTED SHADE

To create a backdrop for the scallops, omit the bottom ring from each column (or just don't pass the cord through it). The scallops will pouf and drape in front of the fabric between the lower edge and the first row of rings. ▷

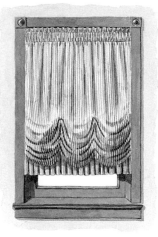

TRIMMED EDGE

You can easily dress up the lower edge of a cloud shade with a ruffle or an elegant fringe. Use a ruffle with a heading or a fringe topped with a pretty trim, and apply it to the front lower edge. Alternatively, insert the trim between the face fabric and a lining. The ruffle or fringe should be relatively deep so it isn't obscured by the scalloping. Apply the trim to the vertical edges as well if you wish. ▷

VERTICAL TRIM

A band of ribbon, braid, or contrasting fabric sewn on the right side of a shade over the rigging rings adds interest to the overall effect. The wider and stiffer the trim, the softer the peak between scallops (or scallop and tail) will be. Determine the intervals for the columns of rings when you plan your shade. Mark the intervals on the right side of the shade, and then center and sew the trim over the marked lines before hemming the top and bottom edges. ▷

balloon valance

ABOUT THE SAMPLE

This printed chintz balloon valance is outside-mounted on a board; the side edges of the valance fold around the board to form returns. Rings up the back of each inverted box pleat are tied together to create permanent poufed scallops.

MATERIALS

Fabric

Thread to match

Small curtain rings

Mounting board and hardware

Shade cord

PLANNING

Read Inside or Outside Mount?, page 94, and Mounting Boards, page 108, then decide how your valance will be mounted. Read steps 1 and 2 and make a schematic diagram for your valance. Refer to Part Three, Basics, for information on measuring, calculating yardage, basic sewing techniques, and hardware.

MEASURE, MARK, AND CUT

Fill in the window treatment worksheets, page 104. If you are dressing multiple windows, be sure to fill out worksheets for each different size window.

Ⓐ **VALANCE** ✂**cut 1, cutting as many whole and partial widths as needed**

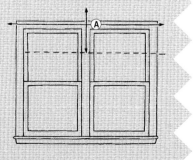

NOTE: The directions that follow are for making one valance. Repeat the directions for each additional valance you want to make. If you are making a valance for a corner or bay window, be sure to measure the width at the appropriate distance in front of the window (refer to Basics, page 96).

1 To calculate the width of the valance, first make a sketch of the window and note the length and width of the wall space the shade will cover. Decide how many scallops you'd like across the valance (A).

✂Make a schematic diagram that includes the desired number of scallops alternating with spaces for pleats; include a half-pleat plus the board return at each end. The schematic need not be in scale; write the measurements on it as you make the following calculations.

✂To find the width of the scallop, divide the wall space width (the length of the mounting board) by the number of scallops.

✂Decide the volume of one pleat (the width of fabric between two scallops).

✂Add up the total width of the scallops, pleats, and half-pleats. Enter this figure in the panel width column of the width worksheet. Also enter the returns and side allowances in the appropriate columns. ▽

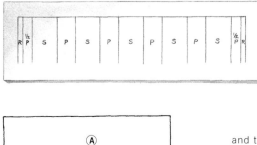

TIPS FROM THE PROS

✂The scallop width is usually 10"–12"; anything wider will be very loose and look more like a cloud valance.

✂The volume of one pleat is usually about 12", which gives a depth of 3" to each side of the folded pleat.

✂To quickly find the valance width mathematically, multiply the volume of one pleat by the number of scallops. Add this figure to the wall space width and enter the total in the panel width column of the width worksheet. Then enter the return and side allowances.

✂The finished pleated valance must be at least as wide as your window. If you're using an outside mount, base your math on the desired finished width; if this results in a scallop width with an awkward fraction, round it up to the next workable increment and then multiply by the number of scallops. Use the total as the pleated valance width/mounting board length.

2 Calculate the cut length of the valance. First determine the visible length. Decide upon the vertical interval for the rigging rings (usually 9"–11"); allow at least a full interval between the top allowance and the first ring. Add two or more intervals to the visible length for the permanent draping.

Enter this dimension in the length column of the length worksheet. Add the top and hem allowances to the appropriate columns.

✂If you wish to make an adjustable shade, just plan for a longer visible length and then add the permanent draping and top and bottom allowances.

TIPS FROM THE PROS

✂Because a valance is stationary, measure the visible length from the top of the board to the lowest arc of the scallops; the lower edge of the valance isn't straight.

3 Cut out the whole and partial fabric widths as needed. Sew them together. Hem the side and bottom edges of the valance, mitering the corners (refer to Basics, page 114).

TIPS FROM THE PROS

✂If your valance will require more than one fabric width, plan the seams to fall somewhere inside the pleat space so they won't be noticeable on the front of the valance.

✂Use French or flat-felled seams so the wrong side of the valance will be attractive.

4 Measure and mark the upper mounting allowance on the right and wrong sides.

5 Refer to your schematic diagram and mark the pleat intervals on the wrong side of the valance.

✂Measure in from the side edges at the top, the bottom, and twice in between. Use tailor's chalk to draw vertical lines between the top and bottom edges to connect the marks. At each side edge, mark a line between the half-pleat and the return.

✂While the valance is still flat, also measure and mark a line dividing each pleat space in half vertically for attaching the rings. At each side edge, mark the line about 1" inside the edge instead of in the middle of the half-pleat.

Sometimes your fabric dictates proportions. On this valance the scallop and pleat spaces are the same width—equal to one horizontal repeat of the large pattern.

jaunty balloon valance

Don't hesitate to cut a valance extra long: The more rings you tie together, the more extravagant the poufs will be.

6 With the fabric still wrong side up, fold it perpendicular to the top allowance to align each pair of pleat marks. Pin and baste each pleat closed along the entire length of the valance. Pin each half-pleat to the adjacent return line. By machine, sew down from the top edge along the basting for about 3". △

TIPS FROM THE PROS

✂ Before basting, test the fit of the valance around the front and side edges of the mounting board. Adjust the pleat size a little if necessary.

7 Place the valance wrong side up on your ironing board. Center each pleat over the seam and press the folds between the upper and lower edges. Turn the valance over and press from the right side. Stitch across the top of each pleat along the allowance line through all layers. Stitch across the bottom of each pleat about 1" above the valance edge. Remove the basting. △

TIPS FROM THE PROS

✂ If your fabric is fragile, stitch across the pleats and remove the basting before pressing the valance from the right side to avoid creating thread impressions along the crease. Use a pressing cloth.

8 Measure up from the hem along the vertical line on the back of each pleat and side return and mark the intervals for the rings. Make the top mark at least a full interval below the top allowance. Sew the rings to the valance. ▽

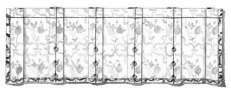

TIPS FROM THE PROS

✂ The stitches will show on the front. Use doubled heavy-duty thread that matches and make neat stitches. A buttonhole stitch is strongest (refer to Basics, page 118). If you've lined your valance, be sure to sew through all layers.

✂ If you prefer to use ring tape, sew the rings, not the tape, to the valance to avoid creating vertical rows of stitching on the front.

✂ Iron-on ring tape is an alternative; test it first on a scrap of your fabric.

9 Cut a shade cord for each column of rings. To create the permanent scallop, thread a cord through the rings in each column and tie the cord to itself around the rings; leave the excess cord so you can adjust the scallop drape later. ▽

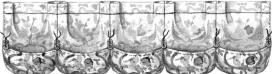

10 Referring to Basics, page 109, attach the valance to the mounting board. Install the mounting board.

✂ If you are making an adjustable shade, refer to Basics, pages 108–110, to rig it.

TIPS FROM THE PROS

✂ The sides of balloon valances and shades sometimes pull away from the sides of the window. To prevent this, suspend a thin dowel (the same length as the mounting board) across the back, below the bottom row of rings: Glue a fabric cover around the dowel; sew a ribbon loop beneath each bottom ring; slide the dowel through the loops.

NOTE: The directions that follow are for making one shade. Repeat the directions for each additional shade you want to make.

TIPS FROM THE PROS

✂ You can make a stationary London valance following these same directions. Instead of rigging the shade through screw eyes, just thread the cords through the rings, pull the cords up so the shade is the desired length, and tie each cord to itself. You would probably want to make a valance shorter than an adjustable shade.

The clean lines, simple, elegant fabric, and grand proportions of this London shade are a perfect complement to the large window and spare decor; sheers complete the look.

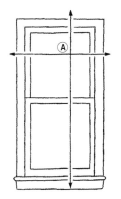

ABOUT THE SAMPLE

This silk London shade is made just like a balloon shade, but the pleats are widely spaced and the side rigging is omitted. The soft scallop and tails are formed when the bottom rows of rigging rings are tied together; as the shade is raised the scalloping and draping increase. This example is inside-mounted on a board; the side edges of the shade fold around the board ends, forming returns that disappear into the tails below. You can omit these returns if you wish.

MATERIALS

Fabric

Thread to match

Mounting board and hardware

Small curtain rings

Screw eyes

Shade cord

Cord pull and cleat

PLANNING

Read Inside or Outside Mount?, page 94, and Mounting Boards, page 108, then decide how your shade will be mounted. Read all of the project directions before beginning. Read steps 1–3 to plan your shade. Refer to Part Three, Basics, for information on measuring, calculating yardage, basic sewing techniques, and hardware.

MEASURE, MARK, AND CUT

Fill in the window treatment worksheets, page 104.

Ⓐ SHADE ✂ cut 1

elegant london shade

1 To begin, make a sketch of the window and note the length and width of the wall space the shade (A) will cover. Also make a schematic diagram of the shade itself, including five vertical spaces—one at each edge for the tails, one in the middle for the scallop, and the two in between for the pleats; the schematic need not be in scale. ▽

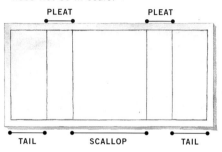

2 Determine the cut width of the shade.
✂ First, to find the width when pleated, add together the length of the mounting board plus twice its width (return). Divide the total by 2 to find the width of the scallop; divide the scallop width by 2 to find the width of each tail. Write the width of the scallop and tails on your schematic.
✂ Decide upon the volume of one pleat (the width of fabric tucked between the scallop and each tail). Write this measurement in each pleat space on the schematic.
✂ Add up the total width of the tails, pleats, and scallop. Enter this figure in the panel width column of the width worksheet. Add side hem allowances.

TIPS FROM THE PROS
✂ Note that the return allowances are incorporated into the pleated width for the purpose of determining the tail and scallop proportions. If you don't wish to include returns, omit these allowances.

✂ You can make the relative proportions of the scallop and tails whatever you like, just make sure the combined widths equal the width of the pleated shade.
✂ On a wide shade, add a center pleat to create two scallops.
✂ The volume of one pleat can range from 12", which gives a depth of 3" to each side of folded pleat, to as much as 24" for lightweight fabric.

3 Determine the cut length as you would for any shade mounted on a board, but add 9"–11" extra length for a permanent bottom scallop. Note the length on your schematic, and add the top mounting allowance and the bottom hem allowance. Transfer the measurements to the length worksheet.

TIPS FROM THE PROS
✂ The length of the scallop allowance should equal the vertical interval between the rigging rings (refer to step 9).
✂ When the shade is lowered, the visual length is measured from the top of the board to the top of the peak between the scallop and tails. Increase the length if you'd like to have more draping when the shade is lowered. Err on the long side—you want to be sure the window is covered.

4 Cut out the whole and partial widths as needed. Sew them together. Hem the lower and side edges of the shade, mitering the corners (refer to Basics, page 114).

TIPS FROM THE PROS
✂ If your shade will require more than one fabric width, plan seams to fall in the center of pleats so they won't be noticeable on the front of the shade.
✂ Use French or flat-felled seams so the wrong side of the shade will be attractive.

5 Measure and mark the upper mounting allowance on the right and wrong sides.

6 Refer to your schematic diagram and mark the pleat spaces on the wrong side of the shade.
✂ Measure in from the side edges at the top, the bottom, and twice in between. Use tailor's chalk to draw vertical lines between the top and bottom edges to connect the marks.
✂ While the shade is still flat, also measure and mark a line dividing each pleat space in half vertically for attaching the rings.

7 With the fabric still wrong side up, fold it perpendicular to the top allowance to align each pair of pleat marks. Pin and baste each pleat closed along the entire length of the shade. ▽

TIPS FROM THE PROS
✂ Before basting, test the fit of the shade around the front and side edges of the mounting board. Adjust the pleat size a little if necessary.

For small, dense pleats like these, space the rings at 6" vertical intervals.

TIPS FROM THE PROS

✂ The stitches will show on the front. Use doubled heavy-duty thread that matches and make neat stitches. A buttonhole stitch is strongest (refer to Basics, page 118). If you've lined your shade, be sure to sew through all layers.

✂ If you prefer to use ring tape, sew the rings, not the tape, to the shade to avoid creating vertical rows of stitching on the front.

✂ Iron-on ring tape is an alternatve; test it first on a scrap of your fabric.

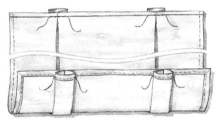

8 Place the shade wrong side up on your ironing board. Center each pleat over the basted seam and press the folds between the upper and lower edges. Turn the shade over and press from the right side. Stitch across the top of each pleat along the allowance line through all layers. Stitch across the bottom of each pleat about 1" above the shade edge. Remove the basting. △

TIPS FROM THE PROS

✂ If your fabric is fragile, remove the basting before pressing the shade from the right side to avoid creating thread impressions along the crease. Use a pressing cloth.

✂ To create an extra-generous scallop, don't sew the pleat bottoms closed.

9 Measure up from the hem along the vertical line on the back of each pleat and mark appropriate intervals for the rings (usually 9"–11"). Make the top mark at least a full interval below the top allowance. Sew the rings to the shade. ▽

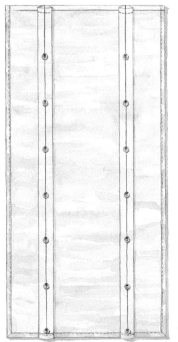

10 Referring to Basics, page 109, attach the shade to the mounting board, install the screw eyes, and cut and thread the shade cords. To create the permanent scallop, tie together the two rings at the bottom of each column.

✂ If you cut your shade extra-long to create more draping, tie together more rings as appropriate. ▽

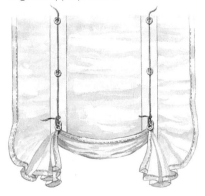

11 Install the mounting board. Finish rigging the shade, passing the cords through the screw eyes, adjusting the tension, and finishing the ends with a cord pull. Install the cleat on the appropriate side of the window.

easy roll-up shade

ABOUT THE SAMPLE

The shade was made from cotton with a woven stripe. The side edges are hemmed and the lower edge has a pocket for a ⁵/₈"-diameter dowel inside the roll; 1¹/₂"-wide grosgrain ribbon loops secure 2"-diameter rings onto the front of the shade. The shade is attached to an inside-mounted board.

MATERIALS

Fabric
Thread to match
Dowel, ³/₈" shorter than shade width
Ribbon, about 1¹/₄ yards
Decorative rings
Mounting board and hardware
Screw eyes
Shade cord and cleat

PLANNING

Read Inside or Outside Mount?, page 94, referring to the information on Roman shades, and decide how your shade will be mounted. Read step 1, and make a schematic diagram for your shade. Refer to Part Three, Basics, for information on rod-pocket allowances, calculating yardage, and basic sewing techniques.

MEASURE, MARK, AND CUT

Refer to your schematic and fill in the window treatment worksheets, page 104, including allowances on the shade as planned.

Ⓐ SHADE ✄cut 1

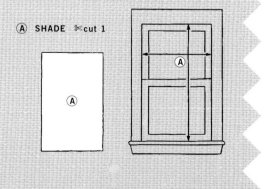

TIPS FROM THE PROS

✄This shade rolls up rather than pulls up, and it relates to the window and the mounting board in the same way a Roman shade does (see pages 76–79). If using an outside mount, plan to place the wide face of the mounting board flush with the wall.

✄This shade can be rolled to the front or back. If rolled to the front, the wrong side of the shade and any side hems will show. Consider using a woven fabric that looks the same on both sides, or roll the shade to the back.

✄If you'd prefer a stationary valance with a rolled lower edge, make the Stagecoach Valance, pages 49–51.

1 Plan and measure for your shade (A). Note each measurement on your schematic.

✄Determine the finished width and add allowance for side hems.

✄Decide the finished length of the shade. Add an attachment allowance at the top to staple to the mounting board. To hold the dowel, add a rod-pocket allowance at the bottom plus a ³/₄" allowance for a hem turn-in and stitching margin (refer to Basics, page 99).

TIPS FROM THE PROS

✄Make the shade a couple of inches longer than necessary—the extra will conceal the rod pocket when you lower the shade.

2 Cut out the shade. Hem the vertical edges and finish the upper edge.

TIPS FROM THE PROS

✄When cutting, be sure to center any pattern so both side edges are the same.

3 Decide whether your shade will roll to the front or back, then mark, fold, and stitch the rod pocket on that side of the shade as follows:

✄Add together the rod-pocket depth and the ³/₄" hem allowance and stitching margin. Mark a line this distance above and parallel to the lower edge.

✄Fold up the lower edge of the shade ¹/₂"; press. Fold up the fabric again along the marked line and press. Topstitch through all layers along the first fold.

TIPS FROM THE PROS

✄Before stitching the rod pocket, wrap the fabric around the dowel to determine a fit that is snug but not so tight you won't be able to insert the dowel. If the shade will wrap to the back, the side hems will add bulk to the open ends of the pocket.

4 On the right side of the top edge of the shade, mark the mounting allowance. Measure and mark a point 7" from each end of the line; this will be the midpoint of each ribbon loop.

5 For the loops, cut two 20"-long pieces of ribbon. Fold them in half and stitch together along the edges, making two 10" lengths. If you wish, seal the cut ends with a liquid fray retardant.

Choose a ring that suits your fabric—glass, wood, and metal bracelets are fine options.

6 Slip a ribbon through each ring, then fold the ribbon so that the ends are even; pin. Aligning the top edges, center and pin a ribbon loop to the shade over each mark on the mounting allowance; topstitch the ribbons within the allowance. ▽

Roll-up shades offer a fresh, easy-going alternative to conventional roller shades.

7 With the shade right side up, place the mounting allowance on the top face of the mounting board; align the marked allowance with the top front edge of the board. Staple the shade and ribbons in place.

8 Pin each loop to the shade so you'll be able to see its position from the wrong side. Turn the shade and board over. Mark a line on the bottom face of the board to divide it in half lengthwise. Make a mark on the line opposite each loop. Insert a screw eye at each mark. ◁

9 Slide the dowel into the pocket, centering it between the side edges.

10 Decide whether you want to pull the shade cords from the left or right edge of the window, and mark that edge of the shade with a safety pin. Rig the shade as follows:

✂ Cut a length of cord equal to the shade width plus 5 times the shade length.

✂ Tie one end of the cord to the screw eye opposite the side edge with the safety pin.

✂ Place the shade and board right side up on your table. Roll up the shade about halfway. Bring the cord down, around the roll, up the front of the shade, through the corresponding ring, and across the front toward the opposite ring.

✂ Fold the cord and slip the folded end through the ring as shown above right. Pull the cord taut from the screw eye to the second ring.

✂ Turning the shade as necessary, take the loose end of the cord down, around the roll, and up the back of the shade; tie to the other screw eye. ▽

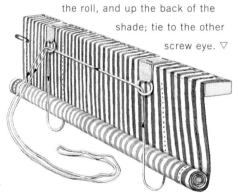

11 Install the board. Install the cleat on the appropriate side of the window. Lower the shade, then adjust the cord loop so that the tension is even and there is no slack.

TIPS FROM THE PROS

✂ If the looped end of the cord is too long, untie the cord from one of the screw eyes and adjust it.

part three

basics

YOU'LL WANT TO GET OFF TO A CONFIDENT START NO
matter which window treatment you are making.
While each window is unique, and curtains, shades,
and swags each have their own construction and
installation conventions, the overall process is
similar for all. In this section you'll find general
directions for measuring, calculating yardage
(with worksheets to copy and fill out), cutting,
installation, and basic sewing techniques. You'll
also find a list of the equipment and supplies
you're likely to need. Whatever the degree of your
experience, review this information as it supports
and enhances the individual project directions.

getting started

DESIGN FIRST

Successful window treatments depend upon careful planning. You might think that your first step should be to measure your window, but in truth, unless you have decided upon the design of your curtain or shade, you won't know which measurements to take or where to take them. Before you begin, think your design through and answer the following questions.

✄What kind of fabric do you want? Remember that thinner fabrics condense more when drawn back or up, heavier ones fill more space. Bear this in mind as you plan the overall dimensions of your design. If you want the open curtains to hang clear of the glass, extend the rod or pole beyond the sides of the window as necessary.

✄What sort of pole, rod, or mounting board do you plan to use? Purchase poles or rods after planning your design but before calculating the fabric cutting dimensions. If you plan to hang your curtains from rings or clips, purchase them first as well. You'll need the dimensions of these items. Read Allowing for Hardware on page 96.

✄If you are making a pull-up shade, do you want it to be adjustable or fixed? If the shade will be fixed (used as a valance), you might not want to make it the full length of the window, and you have the option to forgo some of the rigging hardware. Read Mounting Boards, page 108, for more information.

✄Does the design feature a heading? You'll have to determine the depth of the heading. When you are planning your project, don't forget that the heading will extend above the curtain rod, and that for an inside mount the rod must be positioned sufficiently below the top reveal (recess) of the window to allow for the heading. Read about rod-pocket headings on pages 32 and 99.

✄Do you plan to mount the treatment inside or outside the window? Read Inside or Outside Mount? (below). If you'll be using an outside mount, answer the following questions also.

✄At what height will the pole, rod, or mounting board be positioned? How far beyond the edge of the window trim will it extend? Be sure to determine the position of each board, pole, and/or rod if more than one is required for the design.

✄If you are planning to use a U-shaped rod or a horizontally mounted board, be sure your design includes a return (extension of fabric) to the wall at each outside edge; conversely, if you want your design to hang several inches in front of the window, be sure to use deep brackets, a U-shaped rod, or a deep horizontally mounted board.

INSIDE OR OUTSIDE MOUNT?

Window treatments can hang inside or outside the window frame. Those that hang inside the frame leave the window trim uncovered so it remains part of the decor. While inside-mounted treatments can have whatever fullness you desire, they are usually no longer than the windowsill. Those that hang outside the window frame usually conceal some or all of the window trim, can be whatever length you like, and can be hung so as to visually alter or disguise the proportions of the window.

Inside Mounts

If your window trim (also called the molding) is attractive and you don't want a long window treatment, an inside mount may be the right option for you. Unless the hem falls below the windowsill, almost any curtain or shade design (and some swags) can be mounted inside a window. Of course, curtains hung inside the window cannot be pulled aside to completely clear the glass—they'll stack against the reveal— so lightweight fabrics are the best choice for inside-mounted curtains. ▽

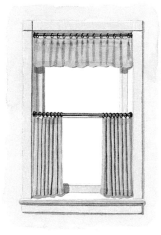

✄Cafe curtains and valances are often mounted inside the window.

✄Roman or roller shades hung inside the window block light more effectively than those mounted on the outside face of the trim, in which case there is almost always a gap equal to the thickness of the mounting board or the radius of the rolled shade.

✄Treatments mounted inside a window do not require returns at the side edges.

Most curtains, shades, or swags that hang inside the window are suspended from rods mounted on the side reveal or a board screwed into the top reveal. Sash curtains hang on rods attached to the window sash—one rod placed at the top of the glass and one at the bottom. They cannot be used on the top sash of a double-hung window.

MEASURING

Accurate measurements provide a blueprint for foolproof planning. Use a metal tape measure and have someone help you hold one end if necessary. Measure and record the dimensions of each window. Even if you think all the windows are alike, it's a good idea to measure each one, as the size may vary slightly, the trim may not be square, or the distance from the floor or ceiling may not be consistent. Use the drawing below as a guide and fill in the dimensions indicated. ▽

✂For double, triple, or other multiple windows, make a sketch of their configuration and use it as a guide.

✂For sunburst (fan) curtains, follow the measuring directions on page 54.

✂For arch-top panels, take length measurements at the center of the window so you can calculate the overall dimensions and yardage requirements, and refer to page 101 to see how to make a pattern for the curve.

Outside Mounts

Outside mounts can be installed in front of the top window trim or above it. They can extend beyond the trim on one or both sides. Depending on your design, you can choose a curtain rod or pole with or without decorative finials, or a mounting board. Curtains, valances, or shades hung on bracket-supported rods or poles do not make a return to the wall at their outside edges, those hung on U-shaped rods or on mounting boards do. Be sure to allow for any extension and/or return at each outside edge when calculating the dimensions of each panel. Unless your design will hang from well above the window, be sure the width of the rod, pole, or mounting board is sufficient to allow for appropriate placement of hardware, brackets, or angle irons on or outside the window molding. If making tab or ring curtains for a doorway, be sure the distance from the side of the door to the pole brackets is sufficienct to allow the tabs or rings to stack off the doorway when the curtain panels are drawn open—or use holdbacks to keep them out of the way. △

(A) INSIDE (SASH) WIDTH

(B) INSIDE (SASH) LENGTH

(C) OUTSIDE WIDTH

(D) OUTSIDE LENGTH (TO SILL)

(E) MOLDING WIDTH

(F) MOLDING THICKNESS

(G) INSIDE REVEAL (RECESS)

(H) SILL TO FLOOR

(I) CEILING OR CROWN MOLDING
TO TOP OF WINDOW TRIM

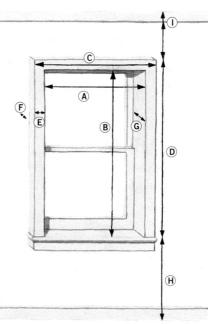

Allowing for Hardware

Before you can figure the cutting dimensions for your treatment you must determine the height and length of the hardware or mounting board. If you are reusing existing hardware, follow the directions below to measure it. If you will be installing new hardware, refer to your measurement diagram or elevation drawing (see Determining Proportions, page 97) and determine the desired proportions for your treatment. Then purchase and install the hardware before measuring as described below. If you do not wish to install the hardware before your treatment is ready, do the appropriate math and double-check the finished treatment before installation. Note the measurements on your diagram. You'll refer to these measurements when determining proportions and making a schematic diagram of your project.

Corner and Bay Windows

Because curtain poles are held in front of the wall by brackets, you can't measure the overall width of bay or corner window treatments on the wall itself. If your poles are installed, measure the length of each section between the angles and brackets. If the poles are not installed, use masking tape to mark a line on the floor at a distance from the walls equal to the depth of the brackets. On the masking tape line, mark the position of the end brackets. Measure each section of the line between the angles and bracket marks. ▽

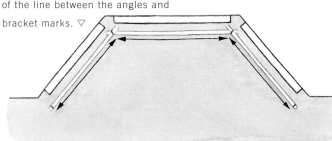

✄For valances, measure as described below for curtains or shades of the pertinent style, but measure to the top of the window opening as well as to the sill or floor.

✄For curtains that will hang from rings, measure from the bottom of the ring that circles the pole to the windowsill or floor. (Don't measure from the bottom of the eyes or secondary rings, as you'll sew these below the top edge of the curtain. If there are no eyes, you'll attach the rings with small fabric loops.) Measure the pole length between the sockets or finials, including any returns. ▽

✄For tab curtains, determine how far below the pole the tab loops will close, and measure from this point to the sill or floor. Measure the pole length between the finials or sockets, including any returns. (See diagram above right.)

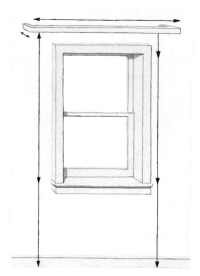

✄For rod-pocket curtains or shades, measure from the bottom of the pole or rod to the windowsill or floor. Measure the pole length between the finials or sockets, including any returns. △

✄For a shade or swag that will be mounted on a board, measure from the top of the board to the windowsill or floor. Measure the front width and side returns, if any, of the board. ▽

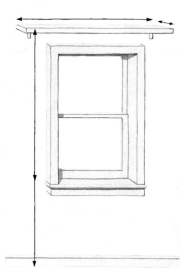

✄For roll-up and roller shades, measure the area to be covered; refer to Easy Roll-up Shade, page 90, or Roller Shades, page 120.

DETERMINING PROPORTIONS

In order to calculate yardage you must determine the dimensions of the wall space (window size plus any extending fabric) the window treatment will cover. Unless you are making an inside-mounted shade, the parameters for establishing the proportions are more aesthetic and visual than formulaic. You simply have to decide what proportions for the design you are making will be most pleasing in the room where it will hang. Professional designers use a scale drawing of each wall—called an elevation—to help them visualize the height at which to affix the pole or mounting board. The length of the pole or board is determined by the width of the window and style of the treatment. Once these are known, the design style and fabric weight dictate the fullness. ▽

If you are making coordinated window treatments for several windows in one room, you will find it helpful to draw an elevation so you can see the relative heights of windows and doors and the spaces between them. This is especially important if the windows are of different sizes or shapes, or if you want your treatment to visually alter the window proportions. If your design scheme is simple, you may be able to copy one of the measuring diagrams on the facing page and fill in the measurements indicated.

Height

For an outside mount you can place the rod, pole, or mounting board at any height you like. (For an inside mount it is usually at the top of the window opening unless you are making café or sash curtains.)

✄Be sure to consider the appearance of your window treatment from the street. Generally, the bottom of the rod, pole, or board should be far enough above the top of the sash to assure that any rigging is not visible from the exterior.

✄If your curtain will hang from rings, remember that the bottom of the rings will be below the bottom of the pole, creating a gap between the pole and curtain.

✄If your curtain will hang from tabs or ties, there will be a gap between the pole and the curtain.

✄If your curtain will have a heading, remember that the heading will stand above the pole, adding to the visual height of the treatment.

✄If you will be using a mounting board, the top of the board will be the top of the window treatment.

Lower Edge

Determine the position of the lower edge of your treatment. Use a sketch to visualize the effect.

✄Usually curtains look best if they end at a logical place in relation to the architecture—at the sill, at the bottom of the apron, at the floor, or puddling on the floor. Anything in between is visually disturbing.

✄Valances are usually $^1/_5$ the overall length of the curtains they top. If used alone, their length should be about $^1/_4$ the distance from the top of the pole or board to the bottom of the windowsill or apron. If the valance hem is shaped, the deepest part can be longer in proportion to the overall curtain or window length, the shallowest part shorter.

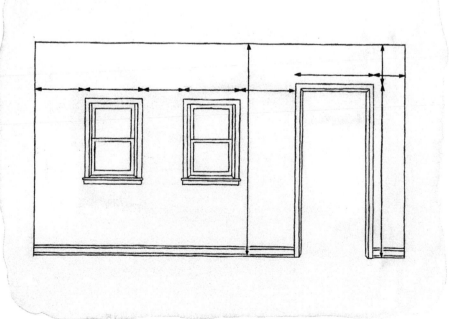

At their deepest point, swags are usually about ¹/₅ the overall length of the curtains they top. If used alone, their length should be about ¹/₄ the distance from the top of the pole or board to the bottom of the windowsill or apron. Tails are usually 2 or 3 times the swag depth. On a wide window where multiple swags alternate with tails, the interior tails can be shorter than the outer tails. △

Adjustable shades should cover the window opening when let down. Outside-mounted balloon and cloud shades can be as long as floor length if you wish.

TIPS FROM THE PROS

When planning valance or swag length for an outside mount, make sure the lower edge will conceal the top of the window opening. For a swag or shaped valance, be sure to measure at the shallowest (highest) point. ▽

Width

For inside-mounted treatments, the width of the space covered can be no greater than the sash width. Outside-mounted treatments can be as wide as you wish, but, with the exception of roller or Roman shades, are usually at least wide enough to cover the molding.

For curtains that hang from tabs or rings, allow a pole extension between the mounting brackets of about 30% of the window width if you want to be able to push the fabric off the glass. Place the whole extension to one side or divide it and place half on each side. ▽

Fullness

Most rod-pocket curtains, valances, and shades have a fullness of 2¹/₂ times the length of the pole from which they hang. Sheers can be 3 times as wide, heavy fabrics 2 times as wide.

The fullness of curtains that hang from rings or tabs varies with the effect desired. When closed, their finished width should be no less than the length of the pole from which they hang, and a little extra usually looks better. Allow a fullness of 1¹/₂–2 times the pole length if you wish the curtains to undulate across the window.

Swag fullness is dependent upon the type of swag and fabric—and because swags drape in curves, extra fabric must be added to both dimensions. The best way to accurately plan a swag is to drape a sample (refer to Traditional Swag and Tails, page 66). To calculate the unpleated dimension of a stacked pleated tail, multiply the number of pleats by twice the pleat depth; if there is to be a side return, you'll wrap half a pleat onto the end of the board. △

TIPS FROM THE PROS

You can make a rough estimate of the width needed for a swag by draping and pinning cording over the window to simulate the bottom edge of the swag; measure the length of the swagged cord and add a couple of inches for seams and refinements.

Tails are difficult to visualize. Make a small pleated sample from a scrap of paper to understand how they work.

RUFFLE FULLNESS

How full should a gathered ruffle be? This depends upon the desired effect and the weight of the fabric. Generally, the lighter the fabric, the greater the fullness. To determine the total length of fabric needed to create the desired fullness, measure the length of the seam to which the ruffle will be attached.

✄ For lightweight fabrics, multiply the length by 3.

✄ For heavier fabrics, multiply the length by 2 1/2.

TIPS FROM THE PROS

✄ The only way you can be sure of the most effective ruffle fullness is to make a small sample using your fabric.

✄ Cut ruffles generously and check their effect on the project; adjust as necessary.

✄ When you are calculating ruffle fullness, remember that the hem edge of the ruffle should fan attractively around any corners. One way to ensure that it does is to concentrate the gathers at the corners when you apply the ruffle; you might also want to allow some extra fullness.

CUTTING DIMENSIONS

No matter which type of window treatment you're making, you must first determine the finished size—including any width or length needed to create the desired fullness or pleats plus the appropriate allowance for a rod pocket, heading, tabs, or other attachment—and then add hem allowances to all edges. If the width of the panels is greater than the width of your fabric, you'll have to join two or more lengths as necessary to create the needed width, thus adding seam allowance to your cutting dimensions.

Seam Allowance

The standard seam allowance for home decorating projects is 1/2". For most window treatments, you'll only need to add seam allowances where you are joining widths of fabric to create the fullness desired for your design. However, if you plan to add a ruffle, border, binding, or separate facing to your project, be sure to add seam allowance to the adjacent edges. ▽

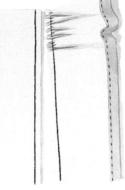

Measuring for a Rod Pocket

A rod pocket is a casing that slides over the curtain rod or pole. The pocket can be right at the top edge of the curtain, or there can be a heading above it. The pocket and heading are usually cut in one piece with the curtain panel. You can make them from contrasting fabric if you wish, but be sure to add seam allowance to the adjacent edges if you do. Read Rod Pockets and Headings, page 32, for construction information and design ideas.

The pocket must be large enough to accommodate the rod comfortably and to allow the curtain to gather on the rod, so the pocket allowance must equal the circumference of the rod plus a little ease; the pocket depth is equal to half the pocket allowance.

The heading can be the same depth as the rod pocket or deeper or shallower, as you prefer. Determine the heading depth and then double it to find the heading allowance. ▽

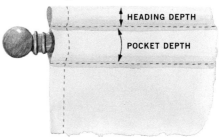

To calculate the total pocket allowance, add 1/2" to the rod circumference for ease; add more for large poles. Add to this the heading allowance, if any. Then add 3/4" for a turn-in allowance and stitching margin. If you are making a rod-pocket curtain, enter the total in the top allowance column of the length worksheet (see page 103). ▽

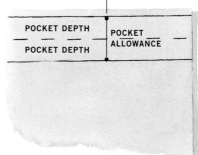

✄Base your measurements on the rod circumference no matter what shape the rod is—round, flat, or square.

✄Sash curtains require a rod pocket at the lower edge also.

✄For Roman shades, use this method to size dowel pockets, but omit the heading and turn-in allowances.

TIPS FROM THE PROS

✄Make a schematic detail diagram like the ones shown here, then enter the total in the top allowance space on your project schematic.

Hem Allowances

Unless your design includes a rod pocket, the top, side, and bottom hem allowances for window treatments can be a matter of preference. Generally, 1"–3" is sufficient for the top and sides, 2"–6" for the bottom, but the fabric and situation may indicate another proportion, so allow what makes sense. When you calculate hem allowances, include a turn-in allowance on the cut edge unless you plan to finish it with a serge or zigzag stitch.

✄Vertical hems double as facings and they'll be apparent from the exterior. Holdbacks or tiebacks may reveal facings and hems to the interior.

✄On sheers and lightweight fabrics hem shadows can be a design feature—but they can also be distracting.

✄Substantial hems may help curtains to hang attractively.

TIPS FROM THE PROS

✄The bottom corners of well-made curtain hems are mitered. Make the side and bottom hems the same depth so they'll align across the miters (refer to page 114).

✄Professionals often make the bottom turn-in as deep as the hem allowance.

Schematic Diagram

You'll find it easier to keep track of all the different allowances if you use a schematic diagram of your project. Schematics for typical treatments are given here; use or adapt them as needed. Refer to page 101 to plan arched curtains or valances.

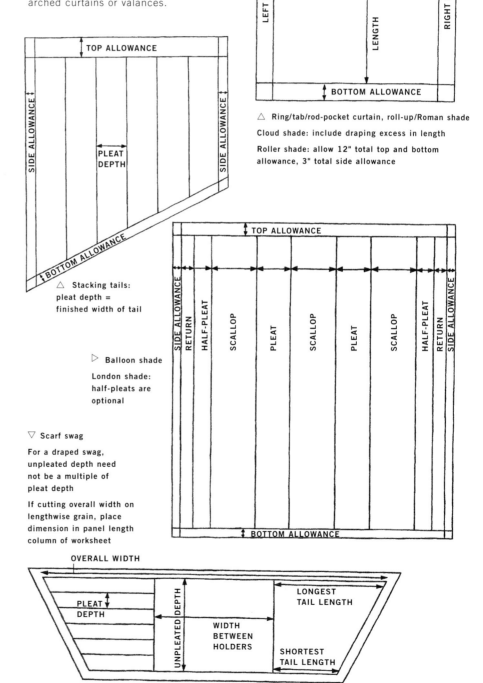

△ Ring/tab/rod-pocket curtain, roll-up/Roman shade

Cloud shade: include draping excess in length

Roller shade: allow 12" total top and bottom allowance, 3" total side allowance

△ Stacking tails:
pleat depth =
finished width of tail

▷ Balloon shade
London shade:
half-pleats are
optional

▽ Scarf swag

For a draped swag, unpleated depth need not be a multiple of pleat depth

If cutting overall width on lengthwise grain, place dimension in panel length column of worksheet

ARCHED CURTAINS

Before cutting panels with a curved upper edge, make a pattern to ensure that the curve will be correct once you've added fullness—an incorrect curve will cause the panels to hang off-grain. Use this same method to establish a shaped hemline on a valance if you are reluctant to judge it by eye. Begin by making a template of the window shape; do not include any fullness.

For an arch top, use tape or pushpins to fix paper or muslin over the curved portion of the window, and trace the outline. It is not necessary to include the area below the curve. Remove the template, fold it in half vertically, and make sure the two halves are identical; square off the lower edge. ▽

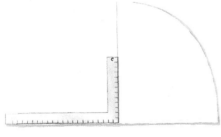

For a shaped hemline, cut a piece of paper or muslin the width of the window by the estimated greatest depth of the valance. Fold this template in half vertically. Sketch in the estimated hemline and cut through both layers. ▽

Pin or tape the template over the window. Decide if the hemline is pleasing; adjust it by recutting or taping on additional paper or muslin.

For either shape, cut the template in half vertically and discard one half.
✂ Decide how full the finished panel should be. On a larger piece of paper, draft a rectangle the width of the finished panel by the depth of the template (if you are making a one-panel treatment that spans the window, the rectangle should be half the finished width).
✂ Using an L-square and pencil, draw several lines perpendicular to the straight top or bottom edge on the remaining half template. The lines should intersect the curved portions of the edge at regular intervals. Cut the template apart on the vertical lines.
✂ Position the cut-apart template on the large drafted rectangle, aligning the outer vertical edges and the straight top or bottom edge, and spreading the pieces evenly across the rectangle. If part of the curve is very steep, split that portion again. Tape the pieces in place. Draw a new curve that skims the curve of the cut-apart pieces. ▽

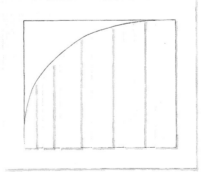

✂ Add seam, rod pocket, heading, and appropriate hem allowances to the new shape as necessary. For an arch-top curtain, add allowances to the top and side edges and just note the additional length that should be cut, including the lower hem. Cut out the pattern on the outside lines. If you like, identify the center and outside edges of the panel.

UNDERSTANDING BIAS STRIPS

Because it stretches, is flexible, and curves nicely, true bias, which falls on a 45-degree angle between the lengthwise and crosswise grainlines, should be used to cover welting or bind project edges.

Bias strips can be used as a single layer or folded in half lengthwise and then sewn as though the two layers were one (called double, or French fold, bias; refer to pages 115–16 for more information). If your binding/piping fabric is sheer, use double bias—it will be opaque. To determine the width to cut a bias strip, first calculate the width the strip should be when finished.
✂ For welting, the finished width is the amount needed to wrap around the cording; add twice the seam allowance to this dimension to find the cut width. If you wish to cover the cord with a double layer of fabric, cut the bias strip twice as wide as for a single layer.

✄For binding, the finished width is the amount of binding you wish to show on the right side along the edge of the project. Binding is easiest to apply when its seam allowance is equal to its finished width. For single binding, shown below, quadruple the finished width to find the cut width. For French fold binding, multiply the finished width by 6 to find the cut width. ▽

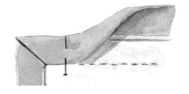

TIPS FROM THE PROS

✄If binding heavy fabric or multiple layers, add about $1/8$" to the cut width of the binding so it will turn comfortably over the project edge.

Planning for Bias Strips

To minimize bulky seams, try to cut the longest possible bias strips; it's worth the results to invest in a little extra fabric. Here are some guidelines for planning the longest bias you can cut from some commonly encountered amounts of fabric:

✄from $1/2$ yard any width fabric: 25"
✄from 1 yard any width fabric: 50"
✄from a piece 44" x 44": 62"
✄from a piece 52" x 52": 73"

Cutting Bias Strips

To find the bias, place one leg of a 45-degree right-angle triangle on the selvage and mark along the hypotenuse, or fold the fabric diagonally so the crosswise threads are parallel to the selvage and mark the fold. You can mark and cut the strips individually, but here is an efficient way to cut large quantities.

Mark the longest possible bias line on your fabric and cut along it. Beginning at one 45-degree corner, fold the fabric repeatedly, aligning the bias edge. Mark strips of the desired width parallel to the bias edge and cut through all layers—pin first to keep the layers aligned. (If you use a rotary cutter and transparent ruler, you won't have to mark the strips or pin the layers.) ▽

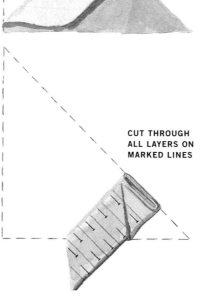

FOLD FABRIC, ALIGNING BIAS EDGE

CUT THROUGH ALL LAYERS ON MARKED LINES

CALCULATING YARDAGE

Once you've plotted your project and selected your fabric, you can calculate the necessary yardage mathematically. Read Understanding Fabric, pages 104–7, and determine the usable width of your fabric, as well as the length of the vertical repeat, if any. Study the sample worksheets, shown opposite. Have your schematic diagram with all the dimensions handy, and fill in the width and length window treatment worksheets on page 104. Label and fill in a line on each worksheet for each component (curtain panel, valance, swag, tail, etc.) of the treatment. If a component features a ruffle or binding, determine whether it will be cut on the lengthwise or crosswise grain and fill in another line for this feature, treating it just like a curtain panel that is either very long and narrow or very short and wide. If you'll be needing bias strips for ruffles, binding, or cording, refer to Planning for Bias Strips, left, and add the yardage for them to the right-hand column of the length worksheet. When your length worksheet is complete, total the amounts in the right-hand column to find the the yardage needed.

TIPS FROM THE PROS

✄Be sure to fill out separate worksheets for each fabric needed for your design.
✄Use a calculator to make your computations. Decimals are easier to work with than fractions.

The following sample worksheets give examples for figuring yardage for four typical situations, all using the same 52"-wide fabric:

Panel A is a little narrower than the usable width of the fabric. One width of fabric is required for each panel length.

Panel B is more than 1.5 times as wide as the fabric. Two widths of fabric are required for each panel length. There will be unused fabric in the partial width, which could be used for tiebacks, trim, or a coordinating pillow.

Panel C is wider than one fabric width, but less than 1.5 times as wide; 1.5 widths of fabric are required for each panel length, and two panels can

be cut from three widths. If the panel were less than 1.25 times the fabric width, four panels could be cut from five widths.

The **shade** is less than half the width of the fabric. Two shades can be cut from one width. If you were cutting 10"-deep binding/border strips on the lengthwise grain, you could cut as many as five from one width of fabric.

WIDTH WORKSHEET

component	width including fullness	+ left side allowance	+ right side allowance	= cut width	compared to usable fabric width*	widths per component/ per pair	x number of components/ number of pairs	= total widths
panel A	45"	3"	3"	51"	52 ÷ 51 = 1	1	4 panels	4
panel B	78"	3"	3"	84"	84 ÷ 52 = 1.6 (2)	2	4 panels	8
panel C	67"	3"	3"	73"	73 ÷ 52 = 1.4	1.4/3	4 panels/2 pairs	6
shade	20	1.5"	1.5"	23"	52 ÷ 23 = 2.2 (2)	.5	4 shades	2

***If the component is wider** than the usable width of the fabric, divide the component width by the fabric width. If the result contains a decimal greater than .5, *round up* to the next whole number. If the result contains a decimal less than .5, you'll be able to cut partial widths for two components from one length.

If the component is narrower than the usable width of the fabric, divide the component width into the fabric width to see how many components you'll be able to cut from one width. If the result contains a decimal, *round it down* to the next whole number.

LENGTH WORKSHEET

component	length (without allowances)	+ top allowance	+ bottom allowance	= cut length (or) adjusted cut length*	x total widths	= length in inches	÷ 36 = length in yards/ rounded up†
panel A	80"	6"	3"	89"	89 x 4	= 356"	9.9/10
panel B	80"	6"	3"	89"	89 x 8	= 712"	19.8/20
panel C	80"	6"	3"	89"	89 x 6	= 534"	14.8/15
shade	48"	10"	2"	60"	60 x 2	= 120"	3.3/4
bias strips	—	—	—	—	—	—	4
TOTAL	—	—	—	—	—	—	51.8/52

***If your fabric has a repeating pattern,** find the cut length and, referring to page 106, calculate the adjusted cut length and enter it in this column.

†**For multiple components,** round up the sum of the lengths.

getting started

Photocopy the blank worksheets and, referring to the sample worksheets on the preceding page, fill in the dimensions and quantities pertinent to your design. ▽

TIPS FROM THE PROS

✄Label each worksheet with the fabric color or pattern name or number.

UNDERSTANDING FABRIC

If you're making anything larger than a rolled shade, chances are you'll be handling a considerable quantity of fabric. Once you understand the characteristics of fabric in general and your fabric in particular, you'll be able to purchase the correct yardage, and then cut and sew window treatments that hang straight—with patterns that match and align around the room.

Grainline

Curtains that are not cut squarely on grain will hang crookedly. Shades cut off-grain will not roll up or down properly. Cording, binding, and ruffles cut on the bias will follow curves and hang better than if they were cut on the straight grain. Some fabrics are printed or woven off-grain—there is nothing you can do to compensate for this; do not purchase them.

WIDTH WORKSHEET

component	width including fullness	+ left side allowance	+ right side allowance	= cut width	compared to usable fabric width*	widths per component/ per pair	x number of components/ number of pairs	= total widths

*If the component is wider than the usable width of the fabric, divide the component width by the fabric width. If the result contains a decimal greater than .5, *round up* to the next whole number. If the result contains a decimal less than .5, you'll be able to cut partial widths for two components from one length.

If the component is narrower than the usable width of the fabric, divide the component width into the fabric width to see how many components you'll be able to cut from one width. If the result contains a decimal, *round it down* to the next whole number.

LENGTH WORKSHEET

component	length (without allowances)	+ top allowance	+ bottom allowance	= cut length (or) adjusted cut length*	x total widths	= length in inches	÷ 36 = length in yards/ rounded up†
TOTAL	—	—	—	—	—	—	

*If your fabric has a repeating pattern, find the cut length and, referring to page 106, calculate the adjusted cut length and enter it in this column.

†For multiple components, round up the sum of the lengths.

The parallel woven edges are called the selvages. The lengthwise grain is parallel to the selvage. It is the most stable grainline. Find the lengthwise grain by measuring two points equidistant from the selvage. The crosswise grain is perpendicular to the selvage. Find it by aligning one side of an L-square or T-square with the selvage. The bias lies at a 45-degree angle to the selvage. It isn't stable, but stretches, drapes, and molds nicely. To find it, align one leg of a 45-degree right-angle triangle with the selvage; the bias will lie along the hypotenuse. ▽

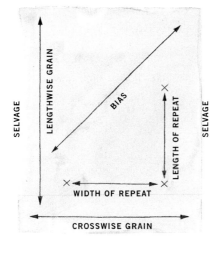

Usable Width

Fabric comes in widths ranging from 36"–60"; a few come wider. Fabrics designed for home decorating are usually 52"–60" wide. However, the entire width is not always suitable for use. The selvages are sometimes so tight that they bind or pucker, and on decorator fabrics they are generally printed with an identification code. The selvages should be excluded from the usable width of the fabric. Additionally, if your fabric has a repeating motif, check to see how far in from the selvage

the motif aligns, and discount the fabric between the match point and the edge.
✂ To find the usable width of your fabric, measure in from each edge across the nonusable portion and subtract the total from the woven width.

TIPS FROM THE PROS

✂ The fabric between the repeat match point and the edge will be needed for seam allowance when you join fabric widths. If it incorporates the selvage and the selvage binds, clip the selvage at intervals to release the tension.
✂ If the selvage is not needed for seam allowance, trim it from each edge.

Pattern Repeats

A repeat is the interval at which a motif or decorative pattern is duplicated on the fabric. Most patterns have both a vertical and horizontal repeat, stripes have one or the other.

Repeats should be matched at vertical seams and aligned both vertically and horizontally from one part of a window treatment to another, and around the room if there is more than one treatment. In other words, the pattern should continue without interruption from curtain to valance, and a dominant motif should be positioned consistently on similar pieces.

TIPS FROM THE PROS

✂ Measuring and positioning your repeat properly and consistently is probably the single most important step in making a window treatment. Be sure you understand the repeat and know how you'll use it before you purchase your fabric.

Most fabrics are designed with patterns that are centered horizontally and repeat evenly on the crosswise grain toward both selvages. When these are cut into equal lengths at the same point on the vertical repeat and placed side by side they automatically match horizontally. ▽

Some fabrics have a pattern, called a drop repeat, that repeats diagonally across the width. These require an extra vertical half-repeat on each length in order to be matched. You must also use extra care positioning the motifs to ensure they frame the window symmetrically. Avoid drop repeats unless you have lots of patience. ▽

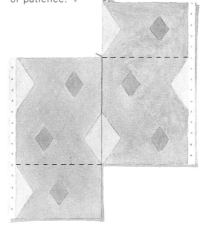

TIPS FROM THE PROS

✂To check for an even horizontal repeat, fold the fabric in half lengthwise and then fold back one selvage; the motifs should meet at the fold in a mirror image.

✂To check for a drop repeat, fold the fabric in half lengthwise and then fold back one selvage; the motifs will not meet in a mirror image.

✂All stripe repeats are not created equal (sometimes there is one color at the left selvage, another color at the right selvage). Be sure you understand where the seamline will fall when you'll be piecing stripes. Try to put the seam in the center of two same-colored stripes instead of between colors. The location of the seam will affect the usable width of your fabric. Some stripe fabrics must be treated as one-way patterns in order to repeat properly.

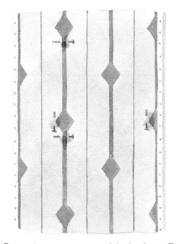

Repeats are measured in inches. To determine a fabric's vertical repeat, find a prominent feature of the motif (the tip of a leaf, for instance) and mark it with a pin on two consecutive vertical motifs. Measure the distance between the pins. Determine the horizontal repeat in the same manner. △

Adjusted Cut Length

If your fabric has a vertical repeat, it's unlikely that the repeat will divide evenly into the cut length of your treatment, so you'll need extra fabric to ensure that the motifs match and align properly. (Plain and lengthwise-stripe fabrics do not have vertical repeats.) Before you can calculate yardage, you must determine the adjusted cut length of each component of the design. To do this, you'll need your project schematic (page 100) and a partially completed length worksheet (page 104). Yardage calculated from the adjusted cut length will be sufficient to compensate for the inevitable waste required to match your repeat.

✂Divide the cut length by the length of the repeat and round up the result to the next whole number. This gives you the number of repeats per length.

✂Multiply the number of repeats per length by the length of the repeat. This is the adjusted cut length. Enter this number in the appropriate column of the worksheet.

For example, if the cut length is 89" and the repeat is 26": 89 ÷ 26 = 3.4, rounded up = 4 repeats per length. 4 x 26" = 104" adjusted cut length. ▽

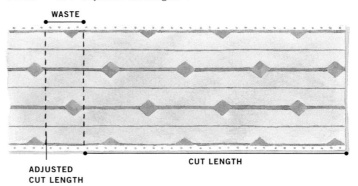

WASTE

ADJUSTED
CUT LENGTH

CUT LENGTH

Position the Repeat

Decide where on your treatment the dominant motif of the vertical repeat should fall. When you purchase your fabric, you must start to measure the yardage at a point that ensures adequate hem allowance below the repeat. If you were to measure from the cut end of the bolt, the motif would fall wherever the previous purchaser wanted it, and you'd be short of fabric.

For curtains or roller shades, the dominant motif should be positioned comfortably above the bottom fold (bottom allowance). This will allow any partial motif to fall at the top of the panel, where it will be concealed by the fullness or roll and be less obvious.

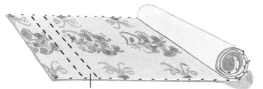

HEM ALLOWANCE

✂When you purchase the fabric for curtains or roller shades, unroll an amount sufficient to reveal the repeat above the hem allowance. Start measuring from the bottom of the hem allowance. △

For adjustable pull-up or roll-up shades, you might prefer to place a full motif at the top so the incomplete motif falls in the pleats or gathers at the bottom when the shade is only partially lowered.

✂When you purchase the fabric for pull-up or roll-up shades, unroll an amount sufficient to reveal the entire length of the shade with the repeat below the top allowance. Working back from the bottom of the top allowance, measure the cut length and then measure the total yardage from that point toward the bolt. ▽

HEM ALLOWANCE   TOP ALLOWANCE

TIPS FROM THE PROS

✂Sketch the position of the motif onto your schematic and take it with you when you purchase the fabric.

✂The scale of the motif may affect the position you choose for it. So might your use of trim.

✂If using a large motif, especially on panels that must be pieced, think through the horizontal repeat to be sure the motif will be centered or balanced.

PREPARING THE FABRIC

If you plan to wash your curtains, preshrink the fabric before cutting by washing and drying it in the method you will use in the future. To ensure accurate cutting, always press the fabric first so it will lie flat and wrinkle-free on your cutting table. Clip into or cut off the selvages if they are woven tighter than the rest of the fabric.

CUTTING

Spread the fabric out on a large stable table, preferably one with square corners. Using an L-square and a long ruler, make sure the cut end of the fabric is square. If it is not, mark a line across it perpendicular to the selvage.

Referring to your schematic or length worksheet, calculate the cut length— not the adjusted cut length—for the first panel. Allowing for the bottom allowance above the squared cut end as you did when purchasing the fabric, find the position of the lowest motif. Measure back toward the cut end and mark the position of the bottom cutting line on the selvage. Using the square as before, mark the cutting line across the fabric. Using the square, check that the line is perpendicular to the opposite selvage. From this line, measure out the cut length and mark it across the fabric.

Cut on both lines and label the panel. Repeat to cut each additional width; be sure the bottom cutting line is always at the same point on the repeat.

TIPS FROM THE PROS

✂Use common sense about cutting from the right or wrong side of your fabric. You need to see the position of the motif.

✂You might find it reassuring to mark out the foldlines for all the allowances before you cut. Bear in mind that you're likely to need these marks on the right side of the fabric when you're sewing.

Cutting Partial Widths

If you need partial widths for your design, first cut them as full widths, and then cut them to the width needed. If you need assorted small pieces, try to mark them all out before cutting any— once you cut a section from one edge, you won't be able to check the square of your lines properly. If you are making a pair of curtains, plan to place whole widths at the center of the window, partial widths at each side. ▽

TIPS FROM THE PROS

✂If you must piece balloon or similar vertically pleated shades, place the seam inside a pleat—but not on a fold.

about installation

The manner of installation will affect the way you cut and sew your design. Curtains and cloud shades require poles or rods and their accompanying hardware; traditional swags and other shades require mounting boards. To install, you'll need a drill with bits, a spirit level, and a sturdy stepladder.

POLES AND ACCESSORIES

There is a ready-made rod or pole configuration for nearly every curtain design ("rod" usually refers to a thin pole or one that is wide and flat). Many styles come in basic lengths that can be easily adjusted to fit a range of window widths. Angle brackets are available to support poles in bay and corner windows.

Rods and Poles with Finials

These are supported by plain or ornamental brackets. Purchase all components together (they often come in sets) and look for removable finials for easy curtain hanging.

Rods and Poles without Finials

Use these for inside mounts only. Two styles of sockets are available to attach them, one to fix to the side reveal, one to the top or bottom reveal or the sash.
✂Tension rods are suitable only for lightweight informal designs.
✂Flexible plastic rods (support with cup hooks) are available for arched windows.

U-Shaped Rods

Generally used only with rod-pocket curtains, these return to the wall at each end and come with attached or inconspicuous brackets. A double configuration permits easy installation of sheers behind other panels.

Accessories

✂Curtain rings and clips come in myriad styles and sizes, ranging from decorative to inconspicuous. Be sure their size is compatible with your pole.
✂Holdbacks are available in U or peg shapes in a great variety of decorative styles. Use them at sill height to keep a curtain pulled back, or above the window to support a scarf swag.
✂Hooks, pegs, and knobs can be screwed into the window trim to support curtains with loop-trimmed top edges. There are many decorative styles. Use them also to secure tiebacks.

MOUNTING BOARDS

All pull-up shades require a sturdy mount to support the weight and tension of the fabric and shade cords and to carry the screw eyes through which the cords pass. Traditional swags also require a rigid support. The conventional support is a piece of 1" x 2" pine board that can be fixed inside or outside the window. The completed shade or swag can be attached to the mounting board with hook-and-loop tape or stapled directly to it.

No matter which style of treatment you're making, the mounting and rigging process is essentially the same. (Swags don't require rigging. They can be mounted in the same manner as shades; refer to pages 66–70 for additional information.)

For an inside mount, the board should be $1/4$"–$1/2$" shorter than the inside window width. The wide face of the board will be mounted against the inside top reveal of the window.

For an outside mount, the board length depends upon the treatment style.
✂For Roman shades, which do not have side returns, the board should be $1/4$"–$1/2$" shorter than the finished width of the shade. The board should be mounted with the wide face against the wall to minimize the gap between the fabric and window.
✂For swags and for balloon and cloud shades, the length of the board equals the width of the finished treatment excluding any returns (twice the width of the board or 4"). In other words, the length of the board equals the width of the treatment on the wall (see Determining Proportions, page 97). The wide face of the board should be mounted perpendicular to the wall.

TIPS FROM THE PROS

✂Don't use hook-and-loop tape to affix inside-mounted shades. It's expensive and bulky, and you'll have to take down the mounting board in order to launder the shades anyway.
✂For cloud shades made with rod-pocket tops, you'll need a sturdy surface to carry the screw eyes. For an inside mount, you can screw them directly into the top window reveal. For an outside mount, you'll need to install a mounting board just below the rod. If you're using a wooden pole, you can alternatively insert the screw eyes through the back of the rod pocket directly into the pole.
✂Professionals cover mounting boards with the treatment fabric or muslin. Wrap the board as if it were a gift package, securing the fabric with staples or glue.

Attaching the Shade to the Board

Mark a line to indicate the top edge of the treatment (bottom of the mounting allowance) on both sides of the shade.

If you are using staples, place the board top side up. Center the shade right side up on top of the board, aligning the marked top line with the front edge of the board. Working from the center to each corner, staple the shade to the board. ▽

✂ For an outside mount, leave any side returns loose at this time. After you've installed the mounting board, wrap the side returns around the ends of the board, fold the top allowance onto the top of the board, folding a miter at each corner, and then staple the allowance in place. ∨

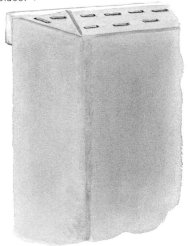

✂ For an outside-mounted Roman shade, the top of the board is the narrow edge. Wrap and staple the fabric to the back of the board.

If you are using hook-and-loop tape, sew one half to the wrong side of the shade. Sew the tape within the mounting allowance if the shade will be attached to the top of the board. Sew it just below the mounting allowance if the shade will be attached to the front and side edges of the board. Staple the corresponding half of the tape to the top or front surface of the board.

Place the board top side up. Center the shade right side up on top of the board. Align and press together the two halves of the tape, working from the center to each corner. Leave the side returns loose until after you've mounted the shade.

TIPS FROM THE PROS

✂ If you're attaching the shade to the top of the board, omit the hook-and-loop tape from the area that will fold onto the corners of the board.
✂ If you are using hook-and-loop tape, you can attach the board to the wall and then attach the shade to the board. However, you'll then have to stand between the shade and the window while you thread the cords through the screw eyes.

Rigging the Board

Decide whether you want to pull the shade cords from the left or right edge of the window, and mark that edge of the shade with a safety pin.

Turn the shade and board wrong side up on your worktable. Mark a line to divide the board in half lengthwise. For outside-mounted Roman shades, mark on the narrow face of the board, otherwise mark on the wide face. Make a mark on the line opposite each column of rings on the shade and opposite the safety pin if there are no rings along the edge. ▽

Insert a screw eye at each mark.

TIPS FROM THE PROS

✂ If you've covered your board with fabric, use an awl to poke a hole through the fabric before inserting each screw eye.

Cording the Shade

Keep the shade wrong side up on your table. On the edge opposite the safety-pin marker, insert one end of the sash cord through the lowest ring. Pass the cord through each ring in that column, through the screw eye above it, and then across the board through each subsequent screw eye.

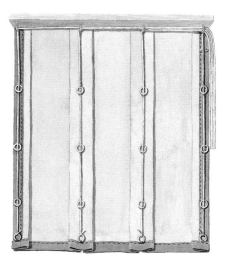

Unspooling the cord as you go, pull through enough cord to hang down to where you'll be able to grasp it comfortably. Cut the cord several inches below the bottom ring and tie the cord securely to the ring. △

Repeat for each subsequent column of rings. Pull on the cords to create an even tension, then pull them all together and raise the shade; knot the cords together temporarily so you can install the board.

Installing the Board

You'll need appropriate hardware and a drill to mount the board. Screws are sufficient for an inside mount and for an outside-mounted Roman shade; for all other outside mounts you'll need two or more angle irons as well. Two people make the job easier.

For an inside mount, hold the top of the board flush with the top window reveal and screw it in place at both ends and near the center, or as needed.

For an outside mount, mark the position of the board on the wall or window trim. Use a spirit level. Attach one leg of an angle iron near each end of the underside of the board and near the middle if needed. Align the board with the marks on the wall or trim, and screw the remaining legs of the angle irons in place. ▽

✄ For an outside-mounted Roman shade, align the board with the marks, lift the shade, and screw the board in position from the front.

Dressing the Shade

Lower the shade. Adjust the cords so the tension is equal and there is no slack. Cut the ends of the cord to be even, wrap with tape, and thread them through the sash tassel. Slide the tassel up the cords a few inches, tie the cords in a knot, cut off the tape, and slide the tassel down over the knot.

Raise the shade. Install a cleat on the window trim at the appropriate level and wrap the cord around it in a figure eight.

If you'd prefer not to have a cleat on your window, try one of these ideas:
✄ With the shade lowered, braid the cord tails from the board to their cut ends, knot or otherwise secure the braid end. Put a finishing nail into the window trim instead of a cleat. When you raise the shade, poke the braid over the nail.
✄ Install two decorative knobs instead of a cleat, and wrap the cord around them in a figure eight.
✄ If a roll-up shade will always be raised to the same level, knot the cord tails just below where the roll will fall, and slip under the roll as a cradle.

TIPS FROM THE PROS
✄ For a Roman shade, raise the shade all the way, arranging the folds neatly. Install the cleat and secure the cord. Leave the shade up for several days so the pleats set.

construction techniques

You'll use a variety of sewing techniques as you make window treatments. Most projects require only straight seams and basic sewing skills. Whatever your skill level, take the time to review the following information, as some techniques may be unfamiliar to you.

PRESSING

Pressing during each stage of construction will result in a good-looking project that requires only a light touch-up when completed. After sewing a seam, press the seam flat to meld the stitches and then, in most cases, press the seam allowance open.

TIPS FROM THE PROS

✂If seams are bulky and turned together in one direction, grade (trim) each layer to a different width. Generally, the seam allowance closest to the top fabric is left widest. Grading helps seams lie flat without bulk so they don't appear as unsightly ridges on the right side of your project.

HAND-SEWING TECHNIQUES

Hand sewing is used for temporary stitching or for finishing. Use a single, rather than double, strand of thread and wax it for better control. For temporary stitching, do not knot the thread; secure it with a couple of small stitches instead. This assures that you'll cut the thread to free it before pulling it out—pulling forgotten knots through the fabric can leave holes or otherwise mar its surface.

If you are left-handed, reverse the terms *right* and *left* in the following directions.

Blindstitch

The blindstitch is used for hemming and holding facings in place, and is inconspicuous on both sides. First, finish the cut edge of the hem or facing. Roll this edge back about $1/4$". Work from right to left. Make a small horizontal stitch under one thread of the fabric, then under a thread of the hem or facing diagonally opposite the first stitch. ▽

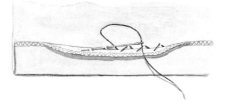

Running Stitch

The running stitch is a temporary stitch used for basting seams to secure their alignment during construction and for gathering or easing during pin fitting. Space stitches evenly, $1/4$" long and $1/4$" apart. If basting to align a pattern, be precise, inserting the needle perpendicularly through all layers and checking as you work. ▽

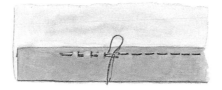

Stab Stitch

The stab stitch is a precise and nearly invisible stitch used to secure and align one layer to another. It is especially good for sewing on trims that would be crushed by a sewing machine. Inserting the needle straight up and down through the layers, make very short stitches; the stitches can be longer on the wrong side than on the right side.

Slipstitch

The slipstitch provides an almost invisible finish for hems, linings, and trims. Working from right to left, insert the needle into the folded edge of the upper layer, slide it inside the fold, bring it out about $1/8$"–$1/4$" from the insertion point, then slide the needle under a single thread of the lower layer. Repeat. When slipstitching braids or other trims, slide the needle through and along the woven or twisted edge, concealing the thread. ▽

Catchstitch

The catchstitch holds two overlapping layers of fabric in place while allowing some flexibility in their alignment. Use it to attach raw or finished edges of facings and interfacings to the wrong side of fabrics; it is particularly useful when the layers will lie over a curved surface. Work from left to right but insert the needle from right to left. Make a small horizontal stitch in one layer, then make a second stitch diagonally opposite the first in the other layer. Repeat, alternating stitches along the edge in a zigzag fashion and keeping threads loose. ▽

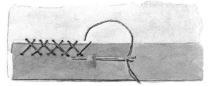

MACHINE-SEWING TECHNIQUES

The directions in this book call for a variety of machine stitches and seams. These are explained below, along with some others that you may find useful.

Baste

To sew with temporary stitches, either to hold pieces together so you can check the fit or to secure two layers to which a third will be added, as when inserting welting. Basting allows you to accurately align seams. Use the longest stitch setting. If you are matching pieces prior to making permanent seams, sew on the seamline. If you are holding multiple layers together so they can be treated as one, sew in the seam allowance.

Staystitch

To reinforce a seamline before sewing one piece of fabric to another, usually so that the seam allowance can be clipped and spread without risk of tearing. Generally, staystitching is done through one layer of fabric with a short straight stitch.

Edgestitch

To secure a folded edge to another layer of fabric by topstitching through all layers as close to the fold as possible.

Topstitch

To stitch through one or more layers with the project right side up in the machine. Topstitching can be decorative or functional or both. Use a thread color and stitch length that are appropriate to the situation.

Finish the Edge

For durability, the cut edge of seam allowances should not be left raw. In general, you should finish the edges as you work, selecting a method that is appropriate for your fabric and equipment—zigzag, serge, fold-and-topstitch are three common options. In this book, the direction to "finish the edges" is given as a reminder only when it would be difficult to accomplish at a later stage.

Gather

To draw up a length of fabric with stitches, as when making a ruffle. Gathers can be adjustable, so you can manipulate and distribute the fullness as desired. If you have a ruffler foot or attachment, the gathers can be stitched to a set tension; these will be even but cannot be tightened or loosened, so refer to the attachment manual and make a test piece.

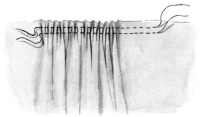

✄For basted adjustable gathers, make two parallel rows of basting stitches, one on the seamline, one just inside the seam allowance. Pull the bobbin threads to gather the fabric to the desired fullness; wrap them in a figure eight around a pin to secure temporarily. △

✄For zigzag adjustable gathers, lay button thread or monofilament over the seamline and zigzag stitch over it.

Pull the button thread to gather the fabric to the desired fullness; wrap it in a figure eight around a pin to secure temporarily. ▽

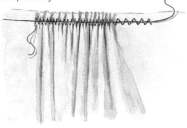

TIPS FROM THE PROS

✄When gathering long pieces, make several short runs of gathering stitches—they're easier to pull up without breaking.

Serged Seam

A serger produces an overlocking stitch to prevent raveling as it trims excess fabric from the seam allowance. A three-thread stitch formation is commonly used as an edge finish. A four-thread stitch formation can seam and finish in one pass.

Zigzag Seam

A sturdy, ravel-proof seam. Place the fabric right sides together. Stitch on the seamline, using a narrow, short zigzag, 1mm wide and 1mm long. In the seam allowance, stitch again, using a zigzag, 2mm wide and 2mm long. Trim the excess seam allowance.

Flat-Felled Seam

A sturdy, flat, enclosed seam that can be made on the right or wrong side of a project. Allow at least $5/8$" seam allowance width when cutting. Sew a plain seam, and press it to one side. Trim the bottom seam allowance to $1/8$".

Turn under ¼" on the edge of the top seam allowance and place back over the narrow seam allowance. Machine stitch close to the folded edge. ▽

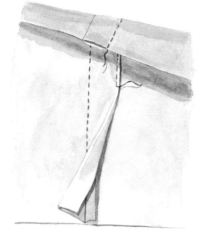

French Seam

An enclosed seam well suited to straight seams on sheer fabric. Allow ⅝" seam allowance when cutting. With fabric wrong sides together, stitch a plain seam ⅜" from the seamline in the seam allowance. Trim to ⅛" from stitching. Press the seam to one side. Fold along the stitched seam, bringing the right sides of the fabric together, and press. Stitch along the seamline, encasing the raw edges. ▽

JOINING FABRIC WIDTHS

When the panels are wider than the fabric, the first step in sewing curtains is to join whole and partial fabric widths. If your curtains are not lined, the seams will be exposed on the wrong side of the curtain and should be finished with zigzag or serge stitching—or better still, French or flat-felled seams (at left) should be made. Place the appropriate pieces right sides together (wrong sides together for French seams), making sure that the top and bottom edges are in the correct orientation, and aligning the edges to be joined. Sew and finish the seam.

HEMS

Hems can be made by hand or machine, as you wish, although for window treatments, there is generally little reason to hem by hand. Because sewing equipment and fabric choice play a part in choosing the best hem method, the directions in this book do not generally recommend a specific technique. Refer to page 100 for information about adding hem allowance. Refer to Hand-Sewing Techniques, page 111, and Machine-Sewing Techniques, opposite, for specific stitches.

TIPS FROM THE PROS

✀A quick rolled hem can be made on a lightweight or sheer fabric by folding the fabric to the wrong side and stitching with a narrow, short zigzag stitch, 1mm wide and 1mm long, on the folded edge. On the wrong side, carefully trim the excess fabric close to the stitching.

Stitch-Turn-Stitch Baby Hem

A delicate, completely finished hem for sheers and lightweight fabrics. Stitch through one layer of fabric in the seam allowance ⅛" from the hemline. Press the fabric to the wrong side along the stitching line, then stitch close to the folded edge. On the wrong side, carefully trim the excess fabric close to the stitching. Press the fabric to the wrong side along this stitching line, and stitch again next to the new fold. ▽

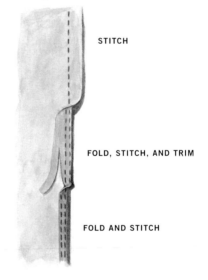

STITCH

FOLD, STITCH, AND TRIM

FOLD AND STITCH

Rolled Hem

Rolled hems are narrow, softly rolled edges created with a special rolled hem attachment or adjustment on a serger or with a special presser foot on a sewing machine. They are commonly used on sheers and lightweight fabrics. Make a test to determine the appropriate seam allowance and stitch length for your fabric.

MITERED HEM CORNERS

On curtains the side and bottom hems should be mitered where they meet at the lower corners; this eliminates the gap that would otherwise form along the edge when one hem is folded over the other. For best results, the side and bottom hems should be the same depth. For sheer fabrics, follow the method given in the Designer Detail on page 44. Otherwise work as follows, finishing or pressing under the cut edges before beginning:

1 On the right side of the fabric, mark the side and bottom hem allowances at each corner. Using a 45-degree right-angle triangle, mark a diagonal line across each corner at the intersection of the lines. ▽

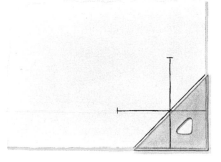

2 Turn the curtain wrong side up. Press the fabric to the wrong side along the marked diagonal. ▽

3 Press up the bottom hem all across the curtain; pin and sew, leaving the miter open. If desired, slip a covered curtain weight (right) inside the miter and tack to secure. ▽

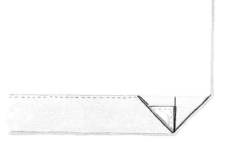

4 Press up the side allowance along the length of the curtain; pin and sew, slipstitching the miter closed. ▽

TIPS FROM THE PROS

✂ You can blindstitch the hems by machine and then slipstitch the miter by hand.

✂ There is no need to trim the extra fabric inside the miter. Should you misjudge the length of your curtain or move it to a taller window, you'll miss that extra fabric when you try to let down the hem.

CURTAIN WEIGHTS

Weights help curtains to hang smoothly; on lightweight fabrics they also minimize the fluttering caused by a breeze. There are two kinds of curtain weights.

✂ Disk weights are quarter-size pieces of lead. To prepare, cut two squares of muslin or lining fabric slightly larger than the weight, place the weight between them, and sew the fabric together along all edges. Sew one inside each lower corner of the curtain. If you'll need more than a couple, make a set using a folded strip of fabric. ▽

✂ Chain weights are small metal pellets enclosed in a cloth tube (similar to a shoelace). Chain weights are sold by the yard. Cut them to the length required, secure the covering ends with a few stitches, and slip the chain inside the fold of a hem; tack the ends of the chain to the hem allowance and then stitch the hem.

RUFFLES

A ruffle can be a single layer of fabric or one that is folded double. A folded ruffle looks equally attractive on the front and back; it requires less finishing because the fold serves as a hem.

✂ Ruffles cut on the straight grain tend to be crisp, while those cut on the bias drape softly, but the hand of the fabric also affects this. Additionally, directional fabrics, such as stripes, checks, and plaids, have different effects when run vertically, horizontally, or diagonally.

Two ruffles can be applied one on top of the other; these can be the same or different depths. If the fabrics are lightweight, you can gather the two ruffles together. If the fabrics are heavier, gather the ruffles separately and then baste them together to keep them aligned while you sew them to the project.

Attaching a Ruffle

When a strip of fabric is made into a ruffle, gathers or pleats are secured a short distance from one edge. The area above the gathers is called a heading.
If the heading edge is finished with a hem or trim, the ruffle is applied on top of the project so the heading adds a flourish; it can be any depth that seems pleasing. Applied ruffles can usually be topstitched to a project by machine. ▽

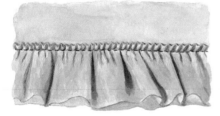

If the heading edge is left raw, the ruffle must be inserted in a seam. In this case, the heading should be the depth of the seam allowance used throughout the project. When you are ready to attach the ruffle, pin it to the project with right sides together and cut edges aligned. Welting or other trim can be inserted between the ruffle and the project. ▽

TIPS FROM THE PROS
Gathers can be bulky. Be sure your machine can handle all the layers before you insert multiple layers of ruffles and welting in a seam.

USING TRIMS

Trims dress up curtains and shades. They take more stress from everyday use than you might anticipate, so select varieties that appear durable. Whether you make or purchase your trims, preshrink them if appropriate.

Joining Bias Strips

Press-stretch bias strips before working with them for easier handling and smoother results. Before joining the strips, check to see that their ends are on the straight grain; recut if necessary. Place two strips right sides together, with the ends aligned as shown, and sew together. Repeat to join all the strips, then press all the seam allowances open. ▽

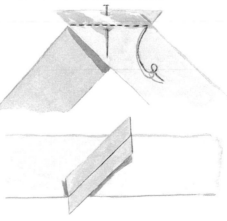

TIPS FROM THE PROS
When piecing striped, napped, or otherwise directionally patterned bias strips, check to be sure that the pattern or nap is always facing the same way—you may have to recut the ends of the strips (to the opposite straight grain) to maintain the alignment.

Welting/Piping

To make welting/piping, put a zipper or piping foot on your machine, aligning it to the left of the needle. Center cable cord on the wrong side of a bias strip. Fold the strip over the cord, aligning cut edges—there is no need to pin. Feed the cord and bias into the machine with the cord to the right of the needle, the seam allowance to the left, under the foot. Stitch close to the cord, continuing to fold the bias over the cord as you sew. Trim the seam allowances to an even $1/2$". ▽

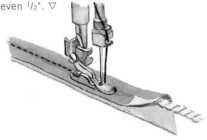

To attach welting/piping, pin it to the right side of the project piece, aligning the cut edges. Position the zipper or piping foot to the right of your needle, and feed the piece into the machine, welting side up, with the cord to the left of the needle and the seam allowance to the right, under the foot. Stitch over the previous stitching on the welting. ▽

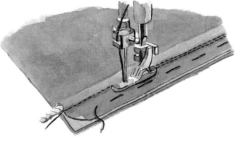

TIPS FROM THE PROS
Use French fold bias when working with sheer fabrics—it will be self-lined and mask the cord or fabric it covers.

construction techniques

To attach another piece of fabric, such as a lining, place the two pieces right sides together, with the wrong side of the welted piece facing up. Align the cut edges and pin along the previous line of stitching. Move the needle position closer to the welting and stitch right next to the previous stitching.

To end welting at a seam or edge, stop stitching just before the intersecting seamline. Push the bias casing back and trim the inner cord. Pull the bias back over the cord, swing the folded edge of the welting across the seamline, and stitch over it. ▽

Single and Double Binding

Binding encloses an edge without adding or subtracting dimension, so cut the edge you plan to bind on its finished line—trim any seam or hem allowance before applying the binding. The bias strips used for binding can be applied single or double.

When binding is applied double, it is sometimes called French fold binding. French fold binding is a good choice for lightweight fabrics. It is faster to apply because the edge that is turned to the inside of the project is already folded and ready to hem.

Applying Single Binding

1 Press the binding strip in half lengthwise, right side out. Unfold the binding and press the cut edges to the center creaseline. ▽

2 Unfold the binding on one edge. With right sides together and cut edges aligned, pin the binding to the edge of the project. Stitch along the creaseline. ▽

3 Fold the binding to the wrong side of the project, encasing the cut edge. On the wrong side, align the folded edge of the binding with the line of stitching. Pin and slipstitch. ▽

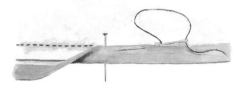

4 If the ends of the binding will be covered by an adjacent seam, leave them unfinished. If an end requires finishing, fold up the seam allowance before sewing the binding to the project. To join the ends of the binding, fold one end up and lap the other end over it, then sew through all layers. ▽

Applying Double Binding

1 Press the binding strip in half lengthwise, right side out.

2 With right sides together and cut edges aligned, pin the binding to the edge of the project. Stitch together, placing the seam one third of the folded strip's width from the edge.

To complete the binding, follow steps 3 and 4 for Single Binding, left.

TIPS FROM THE PROS

✂ French fold binding can be machine stitched to the wrong side of the project when it has been cut slightly wider than needed. Apply and fold it over the edge in the usual manner; the folded edge of the binding will extend beyond the stitching line. Pin, and on the right side of the project, stitch in the ditch of the seam through all layers.

Purchased Trims

Purchased trims, such as decorator welting or piping, cord, braid, and fringe, add a professional touch to a window treatment. Many styles ravel when cut, and finishing their ends can be awkward. Use care and common sense when working with them, keeping the cut ends wrapped with tape until ready for the final finishing. Sew decorator welting to your project as you do fabric-covered welting (see pages 115–16). Cord must be sewn on by hand. Braid and fringe can be sewn on by hand or machine, depending upon the type and the intended use. If possible, finish trim ends by turning them under or concealing in an adjacent seam. Otherwise, use a fray retardant or bind with small stitches.

TIPS FROM THE PROS

✄ The terms *welting* and *piping* are used interchangeably by most people. They refer to round trim that has a flange seam allowance, which is sewn into the seams of the project. Welting/piping can be fabric covered or made of decorative twisted cords sewn to a cloth tape.

✄ In this book the terms *cord* and *cording* refer to a cord that has no flange. Cable cord is the cord used inside fabric-covered welting/piping. Shade cord is the cord used to rig window treatments. Some people refer to ready-made decorative twisted-cord welting as decorator cording.

Attaching fringe: Fringe is held together with stitches along one edge. This area is called a heading.

✄ To conceal the heading in a seam, place the fringe and one project piece right sides together with the heading over the seam allowance; align the lower edge of the heading with the seamline of the project piece. Sew the heading to the project piece seam allowance. Clip the heading at curves and corners as necessary.

✄ Some headings are attractive, and you can stitch them on top of your project if you like the effect. Fold miters into the heading at corners as necessary.

FASTENINGS

For most curtains and shades, fastenings other than hardware for installation are not needed. However, there are times when you may need or want to use hook-and-loop tape, curtain rings, or buttons. If you do, refer to the following to affix them properly.

Hook-and-Loop Tape

Suitable for securing lapped closures or affixing shades to mounting boards, hook-and-loop tape (Velcro™) is available as small dots, squares, and fastener strips, and by the yard in $^5/_8$", $^3/_4$", $1^1/_2$", and 2" widths. It can be sewn, glued, or fused in place. If sewing, straight-stitch along each outer edge. The small pieces are handy for securing decorative bows or rosettes.

TIPS FROM THE PROS

✄ Hook-and-loop tape can snag fabrics—avoid using it on damask, loosely woven textures, and velvet.

Curtain Rings

These small plastic rings are essential for rigging shades or securing band tiebacks to hooks. They are readily available in a variety of sizes.

Use a buttonhole stitch to sew on curtain rings. To begin, take a tiny horizontal stitch inside the top arc of the ring, pass the needle over the ring and insert through the fabric and under the ring, bringing it out just to the left of the stitch. Working from left to right, continue to insert the needle behind the ring, passing the thread under the tip of the needle as shown; a bar of thread loops will form at the base of the stitches. ▽

Buttons

Buttons can be of the sew-through or shank variety. Covered buttons almost always have a shank.

✄To attach a sew-through button, wax a strand of thread, place it in a needle, and knot it. Insert the needle and thread from the wrong side of the fabric up through one hole in the button. Place a toothpick across the button between the holes. Take several stitches through the holes, making the stitches parallel to the corresponding buttonhole. Bring the needle and thread out between the button and fabric. Remove the toothpick; lift the button away from the fabric so the stitches are tight against the button. Wind the thread around the stitches several times to form a shank. Secure the thread on the right side with several small stitches close to the shank. △

✄To attach a shank button, begin as described above and simply pass the needle several times through the fabric and the eye of the shank. Finish by knotting the thread on the wrong side of the fabric or by making several small stitches close to the shank.

TIPS FROM THE PROS

✄When sewing buttons to thin or loosely woven fabric, reinforce the point of attachment by placing a small, flat button on the wrong side of the fabric. Stitch through both buttons, forming a shank under the functional button.

✄You can use a piece of interfacing in place of the second button. For sheers, use a piece of the same fabric.

Buttonholes

The size of a buttonhole should always be determined by the size of the button. Minimum buttonhole length should equal the diameter plus the thickness of the button plus an additional $1/8$" to allow for the shank and a slight size reduction due to fabric thickness. Machine buttonholes should be made through at least two layers of fabric. Often a piece of interfacing or a third layer of fabric should be added. Always test the buttonhole on a scrap of your fabric.

TIPS FROM THE PROS

✄If you'd like buttonholes to be prominent—for instance on plain curtain tabs—consider stitching them with contrasting thread. Or, if you are an experienced sewer, give a tailored look to a closure by making bound buttonholes.

Ties

Ties can be used to secure tiebacks or instead of tabs at curtain tops. To construct a simple narrow tie, cut a strip of fabric on the straight grain, making it four times the finished width of the tie and long enough to make one or more ties; include seam allowance in the length. Fold the strip in half lengthwise, right side out, and press. Open out the strip, then fold each long edge to the center creaseline; press. Fold the strip in half lengthwise and press again. Cut the strip into pieces of the appropriate length.

Topstitch each tie closed, first turning in the seam allowance at one or both ends, as needed. (If one end of the tie will be inserted in a seam, leave the end unfinished.) ▽

Covered Cording

Covered cording can be used as a decorative trim or to make ties or tiebacks. The technique is a bit tricky, but once you get the hang of it, it's easy. Once the cording is turned, you can leave the cord itself inside or pull it out to leave a flat tube. For each length of covered cording you wish to make, cut a piece of cable cord twice the desired finished length. You must use bias strips for the covering.

TIPS FROM THE PROS

✄Don't try to make more than a 3' length at one time; if you need more, make several individual lengths.

✄Making covered cording from napped fabrics such as velveteen is difficult because they stick to the cord, and so are hard to turn. Try using rattail instead of cotton cable cord, and don't cover it too tightly.

1 Place the zipper foot or piping foot on your machine, positioning it to the left of the needle.

2 Wrap the bias strip wrong side out around the cord, placing one end of the bias at the midpoint of the cord.

3 Sew across the end of the strip, sewing through the cord and for a couple of stitches beyond it. Pivot and, stitching close to the cord, continue sewing until the rest of the cord is enclosed. ▽

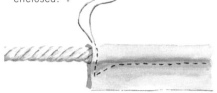

4 Turn the bias strip right side out over the cord: Begin at the middle, where the bias strip is stitched across the cord. Trim the seam allowance at this point and then, using your fingers, ease the bias strip gently over itself toward the exposed cord. Once the bias strip turns over the crosswise seam, hold the cord extending from the open end of the bias strip firmly in one hand and, with your other hand, continue to ease the bias strip down over itself; the bias strip will slide easily over the remainder of the cord. ▽

5 Trim the excess cord close to the stitched end.

✂ If you wish to close the opposite end of the cording, cut the cord about 1/4" inside the end, hand gather the bias covering, and tuck it inside, pulling the gathers tight.

✂ If you wish to remove the cord, clip off the closed end and pull the cord out from inside.

LINED CURTAINS

You can add a lining to any curtain or pull-up shade. Generally, curtain linings are attached along the top and side edges but hemmed separately; shade linings are attached along all four edges. Linings are usually narrower and shorter than the face fabric, which forms a facing on the wrong side of the panel. However, when a panel has shaped edges, a ruffle inserted along the edge, or no facing is desired, the lining and face fabric can be cut the same size and finished so the edges are flush— as is the case with the tapered valance on pages 52–53.

If you plan carefully, you can sew a lining to the vertical edges of a curtain panel by machine. However, doing so makes it nearly impossible to hem the facing edges to the wrong side of the curtain. If this is inappropriate for your project, or you want some flexibility in your proportions or find you want to add a lining after the fact, make them separately and slipstitch them together by hand. ▽

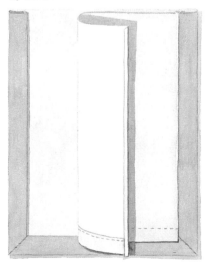

Making a Sewn-in Lining

Calculate the finished size of the panel. For the face fabric, add on the top and bottom hem allowances, including appropriate turn-in, and the side hem allowances, including 1/2" on each for seam allowance. For the lining, add on only the top allowance and 1/2" on each side for seam allowance. Cut the fabrics to these dimensions.

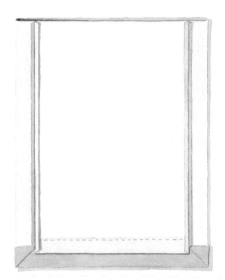

Hem the bottom of the lining, making the hem about 1/2" shallower than the face fabric hem allowance. Hem the bottom of the face fabric, folding a miter at each lower corner. With the right sides together and top edges aligned, sew the lining to the face fabric along the side edges. (The bottom of the lining should sit about 1/2" below the top edge of the face fabric hem.) Press the seams open. △

Turn the panel right side out, folding the side allowances evenly toward the lining, and press the fold on each side edge. Slipstitch the miters. Baste the layers together along the top edge and finish in the manner appropriate to your design. ▽

ROLLER SHADES

Roller shades are quick and easy to make—the only sewing required is a pocket to hold the slat that keeps the bottom edge flat. You'll need fabric, a roller and hardware, and a piece of lath 1/2" shorter than the shade width. A pull for the lower edge is optional. For best results, the fabric should be stiffened; you can buy fusible backing by the yard in fabric or drapery shops, or purchase a shade kit, which will include the roller and hardware as well. You'll also need a staple gun and staples or high-tack (long-lasting) double-stick tape to affix the shade to the roller. Use an L-square to draft the pieces directly on the fabric and mark the hemline—your shade must be absolutely square or it will not roll up properly.

Roller shades can be mounted inside or outside the window; there is specific hardware for each situation. The shade can be installed to roll off the back of the roller, against the window—called a conventional roll—or off the front of the roller—called a reverse roll. Unless inside-mounted on a deep reveal, reverse-roll shades are likely to project beyond the face of the window frame, leaving a gap along their side edges when unrolled. The hardware for an inside-mounted shade can be used to create either a conventional or reverse-roll shade, but an outside-mounted shade requires different brackets for each installation.

TIPS FROM THE PROS

✄The heavier the fabric and longer the shade, the greater the diameter of the rolled-up shade. If your window is over 5' tall, a roll-up shade will probably be too thick to fit in the brackets—pick another treatment.

Measuring for the Shade

Measure the length you wish to cover. The finished width of the shade is always equal to the length of the roller cylinder, excluding the pin and blade. If you are reusing an existing roller, simply measure it. For a new roller, measure as follows, then give the measurement to your roller vendor and ask to have a roller cut to the appropriate length. Alternatively, purchase a shade kit and follow the manufacturer's directions.

For an inside mount, measure the width of the window opening.

For an outside mount, determine how far you want the shade fabric to extend on each side of the window, and measure this distance. The brackets will make the overall treatment a little wider so be sure to leave room to mount them.

TIPS FROM THE PROS

✄Outside-mount brackets will be visible—place a valance over the top of the treatment to hide them.
✄For an inside mount, wait to install the hardware until you know the diameter of the rolled-up shade, then position the brackets so the raised shade won't rub against the raised lower window sash.
✄On a conventional roll, the wrong side of the shade will be visible over the roller. Choose stiffener accordingly, or place a valance over the top of the treatment to hide it.

Making the Shade

Being sure to center any pattern, cut the face fabric 3" wider and 12" longer than the finished shade dimensions. Cut the stiffener the same length and the finished width. Place the face fabric wrong side up and center the stiffener on it, fusible side down. Fuse, following the manufacturer's directions. At each side, trim the excess fabric even with the stiffener. If you wish, seal each edge with liquid fray retardant. ▽

To make the lath pocket, turn the shade right side up. Mark a line ¹/₂" above and parallel to the bottom edge. Mark a second line the width of your lath plus ¹/₂" above the first. Turn the shade over and press the hem to the wrong side along both marked lines. Topstitch along the upper fold, leaving the ends open.

TIPS FROM THE PROS

✂Shades look great with shaped lower edges. Cut the fabric long enough for the shaped edge to hang below the window sill, and stiffen as described above. Contour the edge as you wish; finish with a facing. Sew a channel to hold the lath at the top of the facing. Alternatively, bind the lower edge and sew a strip of fabric across the wrong side of the shade, above the contour. △

Affixing the Shade

If there is no shade alignment guideline along the roller, hold the roller firmly on a table and, with a marker held flat against the table, draw a line the full length of the roller. Determine whether you are making a reverse or conventional roll.

For a conventional roll, the blade end of the roller will be inserted in the left bracket. Place the shade right side up on your table, with the top edge toward you. Place the roller on it, with the blade end to your right. Roll the cut end of the fabric onto the roller, aligning it with the guideline, and staple or tape in place. ▽

For a reverse roll, the blade end of the roller will be inserted in the right bracket. Place the shade wrong side up on your table, with the top edge toward you. Place the roller on it, with the blade end to your right. Roll the cut end of the fabric onto the roller, aligning it with the guideline, and staple or tape in place. ▽

Roll up the shade. If you're using one, attach the shade pull to the bottom center. Install the hardware and insert the shade so the correct side rolls down to face you.

essential equipment

Probably the most important aid you need for home sewing, aside from a reasonably sturdy sewing machine, is a well-lit workspace. However, there are many tools and materials that smooth the sewing process. While some of these are common household items, you'll find that items designed for specific tasks save time and give professional results. Most of these are available at fabric or art supply stores. If you have trouble locating something, refer to the ads in a sewing magazine for a mail-order vendor.

FOR MEASURING AND MARKING

You'll need measuring and marking aids when you are planning your project, making patterns, and marking the fabric. Having a variety of these items ensures accuracy and saves time.

Tape Measures

Use a carpenter's metal tape to measure windows. These tapes are accurate and the leading end will hook temporarily around corners and moldings. Use a cloth tape for taking measurements around poles or hardware.

Yardsticks and Rulers

Use a yardstick to measure fabric width and yardage. Use a yardstick or ruler as a measuring guide and straightedge when marking cutting lines on fabric.
✄Wooden yardsticks (1" x 36") are readily available; check for warping if using as a straightedge.
✄An assortment of metal and plastic rulers is indispensable—6", 12", 24", and 48" lengths are most useful. The clear, grid-printed plastic variety is handy when ruling on seam allowance.

T-Squares and L-Squares

Squares are useful for measuring 45- and 90-degree angles and for finding and marking the lengthwise, crosswise, or bias grain on fabric. They can be made of metal or plastic.

45-Degree Right-Angle Triangles

Made of clear plastic and available in many sizes, these are especially useful for finding and marking fabric bias and mitered seams.

TIPS FROM THE PROS

✄Purchase metal rulers, squares, and triangles at fabric, quilting, or art supply stores, where they are available in lightweight aluminum that slides easily over fabric on the cutting table. The carpenter's rulers available in home and hardware stores are too heavy.

Seam Gauge

This is a small metal ruler with a sliding marker. It's great for marking seamlines and hemlines and for checking smaller measurements during construction.

Pencils

Use pencils to mark clear, long-lasting seamlines, cutting lines, and match marks. If the fabric will be laundered, a regular lead pencil is a good marker. Erasable pencil markers in a variety of colors are available in fabric stores.

Chalk

Use tailor's chalk (also called dressmaker's chalk) to make temporary marks (seamlines, pleats, match marks). Because tailor's chalk can be brushed off after use, markings can be made on the right side of the fabric.

✄Available in block or pencil form, chalks come in a variety of colors.
✄Also available is a refillable powdered chalk dispenser with a wheel marker that makes crisp lines—it's great used along a ruler.

Transfer Paper and Tracing Wheels

These are found in all fabric stores. Use them to quickly transfer seamlines and match marks to multiple pieces. One side of the paper is coated with a waxy transfer medium. A path traced by a wheel run over the wrong side of the paper will transfer marks to whatever faces the right side, so place the paper between the pattern and fabric or between layers of fabric, as needed.
✄The paper comes packaged in a mix of colors; some notions stores carry large (2' x 3') sheets. Not all transfer paper marks wash out, so test on a scrap, try to use on the wrong side of the fabric, and be very careful using on sheers.
✄Tracing wheels come with smooth, serrated, or needlepoint edges. The smooth edge leaves a solid line; the serrated, a closely spaced dotted line. The needlepoint edge leaves a more widely spaced dotted line and, though it may mar sheers, it is useful for marking heavier fabrics.

Nonpermanent Ink Markers

These are felt-tip pens that have either evaporating or water-soluble ink. The evaporating variety can be used on either the wrong or right side of the fabric; it evaporates in less than forty-eight hours. Water-soluble ink disappears when treated with water; test on a swatch for complete removal before using on the right side of fabric.

Quilter's Masking Tape

Use this narrow tape as a seam allowance guide or to hold two pieces of fabric together until they can be sewn. The tape is easily removable and leaves no residue unless left on the fabric for more than eight hours.

FOR CUTTING

Cutting blades should be strong and sharp. Maintain your cutting blades by having them regularly ground/sharpened by a professional; don't use fabric shears to cut other materials.

Shears

Handles curved or bent at an angle allow shears to lie flat and glide on the cutting surface while cutting the fabric. An assortment of shears with blade lengths from 6" to 8" is useful for cutting different weights of fabric and trimming seams. Use inexpensive shears to cut paper.

Sewing Scissors

Scissors have straight, rather than angled, handles, so they won't glide along the cutting table. Use scissors with small, short blades for clipping and trimming seams and threads.

Pinking Shears

Heavy-bladed shears with a serrated edge, these are useful for trimming the raw edges of ravel-prone fabrics.

Seam Ripper

To avoid snipping your fabric, use this handy device instead of scissors to rip out incorrect seams. Slip the point under a single stitch and slide the blade to cut the thread.

Weights

Use weights to secure pattern pieces on the fabric while you are cutting. Made of metal, and often shaped like flat disks with a hole in the center, they can be purchased in fabric and craft stores.

Rotary Cutter, Cutting Mat, and Heavy Plastic Rulers

This cutting system is used extensively by quilters and makes short work of cutting straight-sided pieces—especially narrow lengths such as ties or bias strips. However, the size of your cutting mat determines the longest cut you can make, so the system is sometimes impractical.

✂The rotary cutter looks a lot like a pizza cutter. It has a circular blade that snaps in and out of a plastic handle; the blade can be smooth-edged or serrated. Rotary cutters can give nasty cuts, so buy one with a retractable blade or protective shield, and keep it away from children.

✂Cutting mats are made of a special plastic that is self-healing. They come in many sizes and colors, but all have 1" grids printed on the surface as guides for cutting straight lines. Some mats have printed diagonal lines in addition to the grid.

✂Heavy transparent gridded rulers serve as measuring and cutting guides.

Using the rotary cutter: Rotary cutting is unlike cutting with shears because you always cut pieces from the left- rather than the right-hand edge of your fabric. If you are new to rotary cutting, make a few sample cuts to see how it works. If you are left-handed, reverse the following directions.

1 First mark a straight edge on your fabric. Place the mat on your table, then place the fabric, marked side up, on the mat. Place the ruler on your fabric, aligned with and to the left of the marked line. Hold the ruler firmly in place with your left hand; hold the cutter with your right hand. Place the blade against the edge of the ruler and apply pressure as you roll the blade away from you to cut along the marked line. Lift the ruler and discard the excess fabric.

2 Once you have cut a straight edge, you won't have to mark any other cutting lines. Align the cut edge of the fabric with a straight line on the cutting mat; the fabric should extend to your right. Align the appropriate guideline on the ruler with the cut edge of the fabric. (For instance, to cut a 2"-wide strip, align the line 2" from the edge of the ruler with the cut edge of the fabric—a 2" width of the ruler should overlap the fabric.) Cut along the edge of the ruler as you did in step 1. Lift the ruler, remove the cut width of fabric, and repeat as necessary. ▽

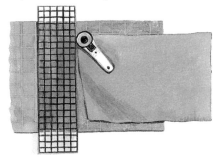

TIPS FROM THE PROS

✂To cut a piece that is wider than your ruler, first mark the cutting lines on your fabric, then follow step 1 above; reposition the fabric as necessary.

essential equipment

FOR SEWING

You won't need any unusual equipment for sewing most window treatments, but the heavier your fabric, the sturdier your machine, thread, and pins should be.

Pins

While you can use standard dressmaker's (stainless steel) pins for home decorating projects, the following are often better alternatives when working with bulkier and heavier decorator fabrics:

✂ Quilting Pins: $1^1/_4$" long with large round heads at the top, they look like long dressmaker's pins.

✂ T-Pins: Longer yet than quilting pins, the blunt end of this pin is folded perpendicular to the shaft, making a T shape. Useful when working with bulky and heavy fabrics, and when anchoring fabric to a padded surface.

✂ Glass-Head Pins: Fine and super-sharp pins with small glass heads (won't melt with heat while pressing) for sheer and lightweight fabrics.

Adhesives, Interfacings, and Stabilizers

A number of products help to control fabric, give it body, or hold it together. Some are used to facilitate the sewing process, while others give permanent support.

✂ Interfacings: These woven or nonwoven fabrics are used to reinforce stress points and lend support to fragile fabrics. They are fused or basted to the fabric and the two layers are then treated as one. Back button and buttonhole areas with interfacing; place it in hems if your fabric is soft or sheer. If you are not familiar with the various types, ask your fabric vendor for assistance.

✂ Fusible Webs: These look like lightweight nonwoven interfacing, but they are really sheets of glue. Place them between two pieces of fabric and press to adhere. They tend to add stiffness, but can be useful for small areas. Some webs come in strips that are suitable for hems. Fusible webs are generally permanent.

✂ Sprays: Permanent and temporary spray adhesives can be found in both art supply and sewing stores. They are particularly useful if you are layering batting with another fabric, as they save a lot of pinning and ensure a smooth surface. Spray them lightly onto the back of one fabric and then adhere it to another. Test the various products (follow the manufacturer's instructions) to be sure you like the way they work on your fabric.

✂ Stabilizers: There is a whole world of temporary stabilizers, which are used to lend body to fabric during embroidery or quilting, thus preventing puckering. They either wash off, tear away, or brush off.

Threads

Pick the thread that matches the job. When in doubt about color, choose a shade that is slightly darker than the background of your fabric.

✂ All-Purpose Thread: 100% polyester or cotton-covered polyester, this thread is suitable for most projects.

✂ Hand-Basting Thread: Loosely twisted white (only) cotton thread for hand basting fabric pieces; breaks easily.

✂ Upholstery Thread: 100% nylon or 100% polyester, extra strong for sewing heavyweight fabrics. Since it's treated to resist chemicals, rot, and mildew, it's an excellent choice for outdoor items.

✂ Woolly Nylon Thread: Texturized overlock thread that is soft and strong, with ability to stretch and recover. Used primarily for serger rolled hems.

✂ Button, Carpet, Heavy-Duty, and Craft Threads: Strong, heavy, cotton-covered polyester, designed specifically for hand sewing. Use to attach buttons beneath curtain tabs or to sew on curtain rings.

Hand-Sewing Needles

There are several types of hand-sewing needles, each designed for a specific task. Most types come in different sizes: the higher the number, the thinner the needle. Here are some you'll find useful.

✂ Sharps: Short needles good for general sewing.

✂ Milliner's: Long, flexible needles good for basting or sewing on trim.

✂ Embroidery/Crewel: Large-eyed needles with sharp points.

✂ Tapestry: Large-eyed needles with blunt points.

✂ Upholsterer's/Sailmaker's Assortment: Large, long, sturdy curved and straight needles. You might find one of these useful for attaching buttons to heavily interfaced fabric.

Beeswax

To keep your thread from tangling or knotting when you are sewing by hand, pass it over the surface of a cake of beeswax. Beeswax also controls static electricity in synthetic threads.

TIPS FROM THE PROS

✂ To augment the effect of beeswax, press the strand of waxed thread with a hot iron.

Sewing Machine

Nearly every part of a home decorating project can be sewn on any standard, modern home sewing machine—including buttons, unless they have shank backs. Be sure to use the proper needle size and type for your fabric—consult your owner's manual if unsure.

Serger

A time-saving machine that stitches, trims, and overcasts a seam, performing all three operations simultaneously and at twice the speed of a conventional home sewing machine. If you are not familiar with sergers, test one before purchasing—and be aware that pins must be removed from seams before reaching the needle and knife. Sergers can also create a narrow rolled hem and an edge finish that consists of small, tight stitches and no visible hem allowance, such as those on commercially made napkins.

Embroidery Machine

Embroidery machines have the ability to stitch larger motifs, such as monograms and multicolored patterns, in unlimited varieties. You can use one to create a custom, decorative trim wherever you wish. Some machines can be attached to a personal computer and scanner to customize designs. Some manufacturers supply sewing machines that have built-in embroidery mechanisms, while others have a separate embroidery unit. Many home sewing machines are equipped with some embroidery stitches.

Sewing Machine Feet

Aside from a zipper foot, your regular straight sewing foot is all you really need for any home decorating project. However, some of the following special feet can make certain jobs easier. If you are unfamiliar with them, refer to your owner's manual.

✄ Gathering Foot: This foot draws up the fabric to lock fullness into each stitch. It's great for gathering long ruffles or lace trims quickly and evenly.

✄ Ruffler Attachment: A large accessory designed to ruffle the edge of fabric in even increments. The density of the gathering can be adjusted.

✄ Hemming Foot: A handy device that automatically rolls the fabric into a narrow hem. It is usually available in at least two widths. Hemming feet can be tricky to use, especially on bias edges, so test on a swatch of your fabric.

TIPS FROM THE PROS

✄ If you have trouble getting good results with a hemming foot when your machine is set to straight stitch, try it with a zigzag stitch. Be sure the resulting effect is right for your project before using.

✄ Quilting Foot: This foot has short, open toes to help you see and stitch along any lines marked on the fabric.

✄ Zipper Foot: A narrow presser foot that sits on one side of the needle only. A zipper foot is essential for inserting zippers and for covering and applying welting. If you are using welting, you'll need an adjustable zipper foot—one that can be positioned on either side of the needle—or a pair of fixed feet.

✄ Welting/Piping Foot: A presser foot with a cut-out groove on the underside that rides over cording, guiding it evenly and consistently past the needle. This foot is a real time-saver when making or sewing on medium-size welting/piping. The needle can be positioned to the left or right of the cord and shifted so the stitches are closer to it.

✄ Leather Roller Foot: This foot is actually a large metal wheel that revolves against the feed and moves the fabric under the needle. It enables you to stitch close to bulky trims.

✄ Edgestitch Foot: The upright flange of this foot rides along the edge of a fold or seamline, acting as a guide for straight edgestitching. Adjust the machine needle to the desired distance from the edge and sew, guiding the edge under the flange.

✄ Blind Hem Foot: Designed for use with a special zigzag stitch, this foot guides the fabric and enables you to quickly produce a nearly invisible hem.

✄ Button Foot: This foot enables you to sew on buttons with a zigzag stitch; it automatically creates the proper thread tension. To keep the fabric from advancing under the needle when using a button foot, drop the machine feed.

✄ Buttonhole Foot: Designed to be used with the automatic buttonhole settings on the machine, this foot is calibrated with a buttonhole length guide and grooved to hold the fabric taut as it rides over the stitches.

✄ Foot-Lifter for Bulky Intersections: This small device is not a foot, but enables your presser foot to ride smoothly over bulky intersecting seams. Slip it under the foot as needed and remove it when you've stitched across the seam.

essential equipment

FOR PRESSING

All you really need for pressing a window treatment is a decent iron and an ironing board. However, there are many other pressing aids; the various blocks and small boards not only help with specific pressing tasks, they can be slipped inside a project to support a small area, enabling you to press without creasing other portions of the work.

Iron

A standard steam/dry iron is fine for all projects. If using the steam setting, be sure your iron does not spit, and fill it with distilled water as a precaution against stains. Place a pressing cloth between the iron and the fabric, or press on the wrong side of the fabric.

Steam Press

This commercial-type press is made in various models for the home sewer; it presses large areas efficiently. It is also good for fusing large amounts of fusible interfacings.

Pressing Cloth

To prevent scorch and shine, place a cloth between the iron and fabric. Commercial pressing cloths are available in fabric stores, but a piece of muslin, batiste, or a tea towel (not terry cloth) works too.

Padded Surface

Press seams, tucks, pleats, darts, hems, etc., on a flat, stable, padded surface, such as an ironing board or a table or other surface that is protected with a thick felt pad, wool blanket, cotton batting, or commercially prepared ironing board pad. A table will be better than an ironing board for pressing large curtains.

TIPS FROM THE PROS

✂Cover the padded pressing surface with heavy cotton fabric, such as drill (an undyed twill weave similar to denim). Teflon-treated covers are nonabsorbent and repel steam, so the fabric being pressed on them tends to lift or shift position.

Seam Roll

Press long seams, zipper applications, and narrow areas over this densely stuffed, fabric-covered roll, which is about 2" in diameter.

Hams

Mold and shape darts, curved and shaped seams, and hard-to-reach places by pressing them over a ham. Available in several shapes and sizes, these fabric-covered forms are either filled with finely processed sawdust or are molded in polyurethane.

Clapper

To flatten bulky seams, facings, creases, pleats, and points, place them on the pressing surface and pound gently with a clapper, made of a smooth high-quality hardwood.

Point Presser

Slide the pointed end of this narrow, shaped hardwood block inside corners, points, and other hard-to-reach places.

Sleeve Board

Use this small, double-sided ironing board when pressing narrow, hard-to-reach places or to support a portion of a seam on a large project. Most sleeve boards collapse for storage.

Pile-Surfaced Boards

To avoid crushing pile or napped fabrics, press them face down on one of several types of pile-surfaced boards. The most traditional is a needle board, which is a specially constructed bed of steel needles set upright in a fabric pad. There are newer varieties, one of which resembles a field of hook-and-loop fastener hooks. Needle boards are expensive; purchase the largest one you can afford so that you can press the largest possible area at one time.

TIPS FROM THE PROS

✂When using a needle board, avoid pressing along the edge of the needle bed—it will leave a permanent mark on most pile fabrics.

Bias Binding Maker

When strips of bias fabric are fed through this handy device they emerge with both long edges folded to the center, so they are easy to press into binding or ties. Bias binding makers are available in sizes that produce $1/2$"-, $3/4$"-, 1"-, and 2"-wide folded tapes.

index

Page numbers in **bold** refer to Designer Details and Design Variations; those in *italic* indicate a photograph.

bias, bias strips, 101, 102, 105, 118–19; bias binding maker, 126; for bows, 51, 64; on exposed curtain rods, 33; French fold, 101, 102, 115, 116; joining, 115; for ruched tiebacks, 39; for ruffles, 114

binding, binding strips, 22, *28,* 28–29, *29,* 102, 103, 116

blinds, *12, 14,* 15, 16, *53*

borders, *22, 28,* 28–29, *29,* **37,** 103

bows, 17, 49, 51, **58,** 63–65, *64*

buttonholes, 45, 51, 118, 125

buttonhole stitch, 117

buttons, *10,* 22, 45, 51, 58, 118, 125

cording: covered cable, 22, 40–41, 102, 115, 118–19; shade, 78, 82, 86–87, 89, 91, 109–10, 117

curtains, 14, *15,* 16, *21,* 107; arched, *40,* 40–41, *41,* 95, 101; bound-edge ring, 28–29, *29,* 96, 97, 98; café, *18,* 94, 97; installation of, 108; length of, 97; lining, 119–20; reversible cuffed, *56,* 56–57, *57;* rod-pocket, **32;** cloud shades, *23;* flat panels, *10;* fullness of, 98; hourglass sash, **48;** measuring for, 96, 99–100; rod sleeves for, *31, 32,* **33;** ruffled, 34–36, *35;* sash, *46,* 46–48, *47,* 94, 96, 100; shower, 56–57; simple, *14, 19,* 30–31, *31;* sunburst, *54,* 54–55, *55;* tab, *17,* 42–45, *43,* **45,** 96, 97, 98; weights for, 114; worksheets for, 102–4

cutting: aids, 123; fabric, 107

fabric(s): calculating yardage of, 55, 97–99, 102–7; choosing, 18–21, 94; decorator, 19–20; directional, 114, 115, 117, 118; fiber content of, 20, 21; fullness of, 98; grain of, 102, 104–5, 114; joining widths, 113; patterned, *11, 12, 15, 20,* 21, 105–7; preparing, 107; pressing, 126; samples of, 17; sheer, *19;* textured, *16,* 18

fastenings, 117–19

finials, 30, 31, *32,* 95, 96, 108

fringe, 22, *67,* 79, 83, 117

gathers, 99, 112, 115, 125

grainline, 28, 63, 102, 104–5, 114, 122

hand-sewing techniques, 111

hardware, 10–11, 14, *17,* 21, 40–41, 94, 96, 108–10, 120. *See also individual projects*

headings: on curtains, 32–33, 46–48, 94, 97, 99; on fringe, 117; on ruffles, 115

hem(s), 113; allowance, 99, 100, 116; mitered corners of, *44,* **44,** 100, 114, 117, 119; of Roman shades, **79;** sewing machine feet for, 125

holdbacks, 21, *72,* 72–73, 95, 100, 108

lace, 20, *22;* marking on, 46, 55; sash curtains in, *46, 47;* swags in, 65

lining: curtains, 20, 28, 40–41, 56–57, 119–20; ruffle border, *37;* shades, 119; swags, 69, 73, 75; tails, 70; valances, 52–53, 60–62, 86

machine-sewing techniques, 112–13

marking aids, 122–23

measuring, 26, 95–100; aids, 122–23. *See also individual projects*

miters, *44,* **44,** 100, 114, 117, 119

motifs. *See* pattern repeats

mounts, mounting boards, 94–97, 98, 108–10

needles, hand-sewing, 124

pattern repeats, 21, 105–7

pins, 46, 75, 124, 125

piping, 38, 39, 115–16, 117

pleats, 14; on shades, 76–79, 83, 88–89, 110; on swags and tails, 66–70, 72–73, 98; on valances, 51, 60–62, 84–86

poles, curtain. *See* hardware

poufs, *63,* 63–65, *64,* 80–83, *82, 86, 86*

pressing and pressing aids, 12, 107, 111, 126

privacy, 9, 11, 12, 15–16

proportions, determining, 97–99

ribbon, 22, 51, 56–59, 64, 76, 78, 83, 90–91

rings and clips: for curtains, 20, 29, 96, 97, 98, 108; for shades and tiebacks, 38, 39, 110, 117

rods, curtain. *See* hardware

roller shades, *15,* **79;** making, 120–21

rosettes, 55, **58–59,** 65

ruffles, 17, 102, 112, 114–15; on curtains, 34–36, *35, 36,* 119; fullness of, 99; with lining/border, **37;** for rosettes, 59; sewing machine foot for, 125; on shades, 79, 83; on swags, *74,* 74–75, *75*

sash tieback, 39. *See also* ties

scallops, 14, *23;* on shades, 80–83, 87–88; on valances, 60–62, *61, 62,* 84–86, *85*

schematic diagrams, 27, 76, 100, 102, 106, 107

seam(s): allowance(s), 27, 99, 111–12, 116; gauge, 122; kinds of, 112–13; ripper, 123

selvage, 105, 106, 107

sewing machine(s), and feet, 125

shades, 14, 16, 94–96, 98, 107; cloud, *23,* 80–82, *81, 82,* **83;** gathered, 98; installation of, 108–10; length of, 98; lining, 119; London, *13, 87,* 87–89, *89;* rigging, 109–10; roller, 15, 79, 120–21; roll-up, *90,* 90–91, *91;* Roman, *11,* 22, *55,* 76–78, *77, 78,* 79, 100; worksheets for, 102–4

sheer fabric, 15, 16, *18,* 19, 20, 100; bias strips of, 101, 115; bows in, 64; buttons on, 118; curtains in, 42–43, 46–48, 54–55, *67,* 108; fullness of, 98; hems in, 44, 113; marking on, 46, 55, 122; ruched tiebacks in, 39; shades in, 77, 79; swags in, 65

swags, *12,* 15, 94, 96; length of, 98; measuring for, 98; mounting boards for, 108–9; multiple, **71;** petticoat, *36,* **36;** scarf, *47,* 72–73, *73,* 74–75, *75,* 108; tied, *63,* 63–64, *64,* **65;** traditional, 66–70, *67;* worksheets for, 102–4

tails, *66, 67, 68,* 69–70, **71;** measuring for, 98; worksheets for, 102–4

tape: hook-and-loop, 108–9, 117; measures, 122; quilter's masking, 46, 123

templates: for arched curtains, 101; for mitered hems, 44; for swags and tails, 66–70, 72–73, 98; for tiebacks, 38; for valances, 60–62

tiebacks, 22, *37,* **38–39,** 65, 100, 103, 108, 117, 118

ties, 38, 45, 48, 56–57, 97, 117, 118

triangle, 44, 114, 122

trim, 17, 22, 103, 107, 117. *See also individual trims;* on bows, 51; on curtains, 40–41, 56–57; preshrinking, 115; on shades, 79, 83; on tiebacks, 38–39

tubes, turning, 33

valances, *23,* 94, 95, 98; balloon, 84–86, *85;* cloud, 80; length of, 97, 98; measuring for, 96; over roller shades, 120; pleated scalloped, 60–62, *61, 62;* rod-pocket, 50–51; ruffled, *35,* 35–36; stagecoach, *49,* 49–51, **51;** tapered, *52,* 52–53, *53*

wall space, determining, 97

weights: for curtains, 114; for patterns, 123

welting, 22, 75, 101, 115–16, 117, 125

windows, measuring, 95, 97

worksheets, 102–4, 106

yardage, calculating, 97–99, 102–7

acknowledgments

PHOTOGRAPHY ACKNOWLEDGMENTS
Part One: 8–9: George Ross; stylist: Susan Piatt. **10:** Mark Darley/Esto; Osburn Design, San Francisco. **11:** Tria Giovan. **12:** Dennis Krukowski; design: Nancy Mannucci, A.S.I.D., Inc. **13:** Alan Weintraub/Arcaid; design: Steven Shubel. **14:** Dennis Krukowski; design: Richard Gruber. **15, 17:** Tria Giovan. **18:** John M. Hall; Bentley La Rosa Salasky Design, NYC. **19:** Ken Kirkwood/Arcaid; design: Lyn Le Grice. **21:** Eric Roth; design: C + J Studio,

Boston. **22:** Phillip H. Ennis; Susan Steger Designs. **23:** Phillip H. Ennis; design: Lauren Rosenberg-Moffit. **All fabric samples:** Michael Chan. **Part Two: 49, 77, 85:** Philip Harvey; stylist: JoAnn Masaoka Van Atta. **All other photographs:** George Ross; stylist: Susan Piatt. **Part Three: 92–93:** Michael Chan.

PROJECT ACKNOWLEDGMENTS
The editors would like to thank the following interior designers for sharing

their work with us: **29:** Patricia Bonis Interiors, Inc. **47:** Jacqueline Rothman Design Development. **49:** Kitchen design: Judy Sobolik of Heritage Design; valance: Rossetti & Corriea Draperies, Inc. **53:** Pamela Bayer Interiors. **55, 87:** Rick Shaver & Anthony Perez, Shaver/Melahn Studios, LTD. **67:** Kate Marchesini, Acorn Design Interiors. **77, 85:** Muffy Hook. The window treatments on pages **43, 57, 61, 75, 81,** and **91** were made by Suzanne Klodowski.